THE HEART'S KINGDOM

MARIA THOMPSON DAVIESS

1st WORLD
LIBRARY
Literary Society

The Heart's Kingdom

Maria Thompson Daviess

© 1st World Library, 2006
PO Box 2211
Fairfield, IA 52556
www.1stworldlibrary.com
First Edition

LCCN: 2006935354

Softcover ISBN: 1-4218-2499-X
Hardcover ISBN: 1-4218-2399-3
eBook ISBN: 1-4218-2599-6

Purchase *"The Heart's Kingdom"*
as a traditional bound book at:
www.1stWorldLibrary.com/purchase.asp?ISBN=1-4218-2499-X

1st World Library Literary Society

Giving Back to the World

"If you want to work on the core problem, it's early school literacy."

- James Barksdale, former CEO of Netscape

"No skill is more crucial to the future of a child, or to a democratic and prosperous society, than literacy."

- Los Angeles Times

Literacy... means far more than learning how to read and write... The aim is to transmit... knowledge and promote social participation."

- UNESCO

"Literacy is not a luxury, it is a right and a responsibility. If our world is to meet the challenges of the twenty-first century we must harness the energy and creativity of all our citizens."

- President Bill Clinton

"Parents should be encouraged to read to their children, and teachers should be equipped with all available techniques for teaching literacy, so the varying needs and capacities of individual kids can be taken into account."

- Hugh Mackay

CONTENTS

CHAPTER I

THE WORLD AND THE FLESH

"A beautiful woman is intended to create a heaven on earth and she has no business wasting herself making imaginary excursions into any future paradise. The present is her time for action; and again, Charlotte, I ask you to name the day upon which you intend to marry me," said Nickols Powers, as he stood lounging in the broad window of Aunt Clara's music room and gazing down into the subdued traffic of upper Madison Avenue.

"I wish you had never taken me across that ferry and into that room crowded with redolent humanity to hear an absurd little man string together vivid, gross words about religion, words that made me tingle all over," I answered as I threw my coat on a chair, lifted my hat from my head and sat down on the seat before the dark old piano. "I think religion is the most awful thing in the world and I am as afraid of it as I am of - of death. I'm going home to my father."

"Oh, don't be afraid of it. Religion is the most potent form of intoxication known to the human race. That's why I took you over to hear the little baseball player. I wanted you to get a sip. But don't let it go to your head." And Nickols mocked me with soft tenderness in his smile.

"Well, it frightened me, and I don't like it. I'm going home to my father and forget it," I reiterated with a kind of numbness upon me, the like of which I had never before experienced.

"I'll protect you from any religious danger just as effectively as Judge Powers. I'm younger - slightly - than he, but I know just as many of the wiles of the world and the flesh as he does and maybe a few more," Nickols assured me, with a flash in his dark eyes that was both wicked and humorous, as well as very delightful.

"And the devil, too! But you don't understand. I must go home to my father," I answered still again.

"You don't understand yourself," returned Nickols. "There are strange hieroglyphics imprinted on every woman's heart and a man can read only an unconnected word here and there when he can get his flashlight thrown into the depths - if he dares adventure into her life at all. I feel that I take my own life in my hands when I allow you to talk to me as I am allowing you to-night."

"How do you know that those hieroglyphics might not mean the salvation of the world if she could spell them out herself, or some great and good person took a steady lamp and went down into her heart and -"

"It takes a very wicked man to read a woman; good men are blinded by them and stumble," Nickols assured me as he came over, stood beside me and ran his long, slender, artist's fingers up and down the keys of the piano, which evoked a strange, diabolical sort of harmony from them. "I understand about it all, so please come tell me you'll marry me." This time his arms almost encircled me, but I slipped between them as he laughed at me with his adorable pagan charm.

"No, Nickols, that would be an easy - and - and delightful way out, but I am really frightened down in some queer part of my anatomy that lies between my breast bone and my spinal column. Something is stirring in my heart and I'm afraid of it. I've got to get out in a wilderness and fight with it."

"Take it out on me," offered Nickols, with a laugh that was both wistful and provoking.

"No, I've got a home panic and I must go."

"Then when do I get my answer from what is left of you after the battle?"

"I'll let you know when to come and get it - under the roof of the Poplars," I answered him from the doorway.

And the very next morning I went down into the Harpeth Valley, driven I knew not by what, nor to what. I only knew that I felt full of a living, smothered flame and I was sure that it was best to let it burst forth in my ancestral abiding place.

I was born of a man who has the most evolved brain in the Harpeth Valley, who has been a drunkard for twenty years, and of a very beautiful and haughty woman whose own mother, to the day of her death, shouted at Methodist love feasts. Is it any wonder that when I was tried by fire I burned "as the cracklings of thorns under a pot?"

"How *could* you set that ridiculous little Methodist meeting house on the very doorstep of my garden, father?" I demanded, as I stood tall and furious before him in the breakfast room on the morning after my return home from my winter in the East with Aunt Clara. "Cousin Nickols has spent many months out of three years on the plans of restoration for that garden, and he is coming down soon to sketch and photograph it to use in some of his commissions. What shall I - what will *you* - say to him when he finds that the vista he kept open for the line of Paradise Ridge has been cut off by that pile of stones to house the singing of psalms?" And as I raged I had a feeling of being relentlessly pursued - by something I didn't understand.

"Madam," returned father, with a dignity he always used with me when he encountered one of my rages, "you will find that the chapel does not in any way interfere with Nickols' carefully planned view. Gregory Goodloe spent many days of thought in seeking to place it so that it would not intrude itself upon your garden, and he built his parsonage completely out of view, though it gives him only one large southern window to his study and only northern ones to his bedroom."

"Does the creature also sleep and eat and have his being right there behind my hollyhocks?" I demanded, and my rage began to merge into actual grief, which in turn threatened to come to the surface in hot tears.

"Now, Charlotte, my daughter," father was beginning to say with soothing in his voice instead of the belligerence that from my youth up had always just preceded my floods of tears. Dabney, the shriveled black butler, who had always devotedly sympathized with my exhibitions of temperament, to which he had, from my infancy, given the name of "tantrums," set the platter of fried chicken before father's place at the damask and silver-spread old table by the window, through which the morning sun was shining genially. Then, with a smile as broad and genial as that of the sun, he drew out my chair from behind the ancestral silver coffee urn, which was puffing out clouds of fragrant steam.

"Breakfast am sarved, honey chile," he crooned soothingly, "an' yo' Mammy done put the liver wing right ag'in yo' fork."

Dabney had many times stemmed my floods with choice food and was trying his favorite method of pacification.

I faltered and wavered at the temptation. I was hungry.

"Just wait until you see Goodloe and talk it over with him," father said, as he seized the advantage of my wavering and seated himself opposite me as Dabney pushed in my chair and whisked the cover off the silver sugar bowl and presented one of his old willow-ware cups for father's two lumps and a dash of cream. "I asked him to -"

"See him? You don't expect me to discuss Nickols' and my garden with an ignorant bucolic Methodist minister, who probably doesn't know a honeysuckle from a jimson weed, do you?" I asked with actual rage rising again above the tears as I literally dashed the cream into his cup and deluged the boiling coffee down upon it so that a scalding splatter peppered my hand. "I never want to see or hear or speak to or about him. I'll build a trellis as high as his church, run evergreen honeysuckle on it and go my way in an opposite direction from his. I'll - " Just here I observed consternation spread over Dabney's black face, then communicate itself to father's distressed countenance as he glanced out the window. Quickly he pushed his morning julep behind the jar of roses in the center of the table, while Dabney flung a napkin over the silver pitcher with frost on its sides and mint nodding over its brim.

And then, as I was about to pour my own coffee and launch forth on another tirade on the subject of my neighbor, I heard a rich tenor voice singing just outside the window in the garden beside the steps that led down from the long windows in the dining room to the old flagstone walk. Nickols and I had searched through volumes of dusty antique prints to see just how we wanted that walk to lead out to the sunken garden beyond the tall old poplars. I also saw the handle of a rake or hoe in action across the window landscape and heard unmistakable sounds of vigorous gardening.

I rose to my feet with battle in my eyes and then stopped perfectly still and listened - unwillingly but compelled.

"Drink to me only with thine eyes
And I will pledge with mine,"

were the words that floated in at the window on the fragrant morning sunbeams, in a voice of the most penetrating tenderness I had ever felt break against my heartstrings.

"I - I - he sometimes demolishes a - a few weeds," father faltered, while Dabney ducked his cotton-wool old head and slipped out of the door.

"You allow him to work in my - garden - and -" I faltered, just recovering from the impact of the words of my favorite song of songs hurled at me by the unseen enemy, when I was interrupted by his appearance in the open door and we stood facing each other.

I am a woman who has very decided tastes about the biological man. I know just how I want the creatures to look, and I haven't much interest in one that isn't at least of the type of my preferred kind. Because I am very tall and broad and deep-bosomed and vivid and high colored, and have strong white teeth that crunch up about as much food in the twenty-four hours as most field hands consume, and altogether I am very much like one of the most vigorous of Sorolla's paintings, that is the probable pathological reason I have always preferred an evolved Whistler masculine nocturne that retreats to the limits of my comprehension and then beckons me to follow. All other men I have grouped beyond the border of my feminine nature and sought to waste no thought upon them. It was a shock to come, suddenly, in my own breakfast room, face to face with a type of man I had never before met. The enemy was astonishingly large and lithe and distinctly resembled one of the big gold-colored lions that live in the wilds of the Harpeth Mountains out beyond Paradise Ridge. His head, with its tawny thatch that ought to have waved majestically but which was sleek and decorous to the point of worldliness, was poised on his neck and shoulders with a singularly strong line that showed through a silk soft collar, held together by an exquisitely worldly amethyst silk scarf which, it was a shock to see, matched glints from eyes back under his heavy gold brows with what appeared to be extreme sophistication. After the shock of the tie the loose gray London worsted coat and trousers made only a passing impression; and from my involuntary summary of the whole surprising man, which had taken less than an instant, my dazed brain came back and was held and concentrated by the beauty of the smile that flooded out over me in welcome after my father's hurried introduction.

Maria Thompson Daviess

"The Reverend Mr. Gregory Goodloe - my daughter Charlotte," father announced, as he rose and waved in my direction a hand that was cordial to the point of bravado.

"I'm so glad you came in time to see your crocuses and anemones, Miss Powers," the Jaguar said as he took my hand in his. "Dabney has let me help him hand-weed them and they are a glory, aren't they?" While he spoke he still held my hand and I was still too dazed to regain possession of it. Father saved the situation.

"Sit down, sit down, Parson, and let Charlotte give you a cup of coffee while it is on the simmer," he urged with hasty hospitality as if intent upon effectively bottling me up, at least for the immediate present. "She was just pouring my cup. Will you say grace before I take my first sip?" was the high explosive he further proceeded to hurl in my face.

And as he spoke I sank dumbly into my chair and helplessly bowed my head to a ceremony so obsolete in the world from which I had come that I felt as if I was slipping back into the days of the pioneer, when the customs of life were still primitive and dictated by emotion rather than mental science.

And there, with father's concealed mint julep right against his interlaced fingers, the mountain lion bowed his crested head and involved me in prayer for the first time since chapel-service in my college days.

"The earth is the Lord's and the fullness thereof ... for which we give thanks, thy children, with Lord Jesus, Amen!"

"Amen," mumbled father as if from the depths of embarrass-ment, and against my will, as it were, a queer sort of a croon of an echo came from my own throat.

Also that was the first time I had ever heard words of prayer under the roof of the Poplars. It embarrassed me and I hated it and the cause of it. The spell which had possessed me since the entrance of the Reverend Goodloe, vanished, and the rage that had been in me at the discovery of the intrusion of his chapel and himself upon my life when I had come home to be free to be wicked, boiled up within me and then sugared down to a rich - and dangerous - syrup. While I poured his coffee I again took stock of him, this time coldly and with deadly intent. The reasons for his entry into my hitherto satisfactory family life, even at breakfast time, I did not know, any more than I knew the reason for the chapel on the other side of the hollyhocks, but I felt that I feared both and intended to get rid of them. If the enemy had been what one could reasonably expect a young Methodist preacher to be, I would have routed him and his meekness within the hour and had the chapel moved to a lot on a side street in town within the week. However, when a hunter comes suddenly upon a Harpeth jaguar he is glad to use his best repeater and he is careful how he shoots, though if he is very skillful he may tease the lion aloft with a few nipping shots. I felt suddenly very strong for the fight that I knew was on, though the lion didn't possess that knowledge as yet. Deliberately I fired a preliminary bullet that seemed to graze father, though it left the Parson unharmed.

"Will you have your mint julep before I pour your coffee, Mr. Goodloe?" I asked, with seemingly careless friendliness. "Dabney, put fresh ice in father's glass and fill mine and Mr. Goodloe's."

"I was feeling a little under the weather this morning," said father hastily, as he set his glass from behind the rose jar upon Dabney's waiter and motioned it all away from him, thus denying the morning friend of his lifetime. I had never drunk a julep before breakfast in my life, only tasted around the frosty edges of father's, but I held my ground, and held out my glass to Dabney, who falteringly, almost in terror, took the frosted silver pitcher from the sideboard and poured me an unusually large draft of the family beverage.

"Will you have yours now, Mr. Goodloe?" I asked again with still more of the sugared solicitation.

Maria Thompson Daviess

"No, I believe I prefer the coffee, but don't pour it until you have drunk your julep; you know frost is a thing that soon passes," was the cheerful answer, though a suspicion of an amethyst glint made me know that the Jaguar had at least heard the zip of the bullet.

I loathed that mixture of ice and sugar and mint and whiskey but I had to drink it, and it heated me up inside both physically and mentally, and took away all the queer dogging fear. And because of it I don't remember what else happened at that breakfast except that I wanted to clutch and cling to the warm, strong hand that I again found mine in at the time of parting. But I didn't; at least, I don't think I did. After it was taken away from me I went very slowly up to my room and again went to bed, Mammy caressingly officiating and rejoicing that I was going to "nap the steam cars outen my bones."

I fell asleep with the continued strains of "Drink to me only" in my ears, and wondering if I ought to put it down as insult added to injury, and I awoke several hours later to find Letitia Cockrell, one of the dear friends whom many generations had bestowed upon me, sitting on the foot of my bed consuming the last of the box of marrons with which Nickols had provisioned my journey down from New York. I was glad I had tucked the note that came in the box under my pillow the night before. I trust Letitia and she is entirely sophisticated, but she has never had a lover who lives in Greenwich Village, New York, America.

"Is this the open season for two-day hangovers, in New York?" she demanded as she sniffed me suspiciously at the same time she dimpled and smiled at me.

"No, this is not a metropolitan hangover. It was acquired at breakfast, Letitia," I answered her as I sat up and stretched out my bare arms to give her a good shake and a hug. "'You may break, you may shatter the glass if you will, but the scent of the julep will hang 'round you still,'" I misquoted as I drew my knees up into my embrace and took the last remaining marron.

"Why, Mammy said Mr. Goodloe had breakfast with you. Did you sneak it from the judge's pitcher?" demanded Letitia, as she likewise drew her knees up into her arms and settled herself against one of the posts of my bed for the many hours' resume of our individual existences in which we always indulged upon being reunited after separation.

"I did not," I answered. "I drank it before his eyes, and then I don't remember what happened and I don't care."

"What?"

"Just that. I never have been drunk because I never could drink enough. I've always felt that there isn't enough liquid in the world to faze me, and I don't like it anyway, but Dabney was so impressed by His Worship that he poured it double for me before I had had breakfast. I hope I staggered or swore but I don't think I did. The Reverend Goodloe can tell you better than I. Ask him."

"Gregory Goodloe? Oh, Charlotte!"

"That's the point I was coming to, Letitia: Just who is this Reverend Goodloe that I shouldn't drink a quart of mint julep before him if I want to? I had well over a pint of champagne with a Mr. Justice two nights before I left New York and I stopped then out of courtesy to one of the generals whom we expect to defend us from the Kaiser. Who is your Gregory Goodloe? Tell we all about him, unexpurgated and unafraid."

"Didn't you know about him - and the chapel before you came?" Letitia queried cautiously, as if fearing the explosion she felt was sure to result.

"I did not," I answered. "I met him and his chapel and the mint julep all in the same five minutes, and is it any wonder I went down? Go on. Tell me the worst or the best. I'm ready."

Maria Thompson Daviess

And as I spoke I settled my pillows comfortably, getting a little thrill from the crumpled letter underneath the bottom one.

CHAPTER II

THE HARPETH JAGUAR

"It is beautifully romantic, but I don't know what we are going to do about it," answered Letitia with genuine trouble, puckering her brow under one of her smooth waves of seal-brown hair. Letitia is one of the wonderful variety of women who patch out life, piece by piece, in a beautiful symmetrical pattern and who do not have imagination enough to admire anything about a riotous crazy quilt. She is in love with Clifton Gray, has been since she wound her brown braids about her head, and is piecing strips of him into her life-fabric by the very sanest love - courtship - marriage design.

"We just can't go on as we have been doing lately," she continued. "We all decided that you would know what to do about him, and would do it when you came home. We suspected Judge Powers hadn't written you all the facts when you didn't come and the building went on up. You will be able to do something about him, won't you?"

"I think it is likely," I answered, with the brittle sugar in my voice that Letitia only half knows the flavor of. "But don't try to sketch things, Letitia. Begin at the beginning and go straight to the end; I'll pick up the pieces."

"Well, of course you remember the Bishop Goodloe romance, don't you?" asked Letitia, hopeful that she could get a small start ahead on her chronicle.

"I don't remember anything about any bishop, ever. I forget things about that kind of people. What did, or didn't he do?"

"Charlotte!" remonstrated Letitia. "He was the last of the Goodloes who built that old Goodloe home on exactly the place where the first Goodloe set the stakes of the first stockade put up in the Harpeth Valley, right here in Goodloets. It burned down the night he married that Miss Gregory in New York, before we were born. Don't you remember we used to play in the ruins, just over here beyond the garden where the chapel stands now? Your father bought the property. Part of your garden is old Madam Goodloe's garden and that's why it was so wonderful for Judge Powers to give the lot and let Mr. Goodloe build the chapel there. We all felt that, though some of us were scared when we thought about what you might do when you came home. Still, after we saw that wonderful little stone chapel that Mr. Goodloe had one of the greatest architects in New York design, after he had sent him packages of sketches of your garden and the Poplars, so it would only make it all the more beautiful, we felt better. You don't really mind about it, do you, dear?" Letitia's voice was beseechingly enthusiastic, though keyed down with a note of anxiety.

"Go on!" I commanded, packing down the rage in the dark corners of my inmost heart.

"Nobody ever knew why Bishop Goodloe never came back after he married while on a mission from the Southern Methodist Conference to the Northern Methodist Conference. He severed his relations with his own Conference, and he never preached again though he was one of the most wonderful and eloquent preachers the South has ever known. He was the youngest bishop the church had ever ordained. Nobody ever knew what happened, and all we know now is that this perfectly beautiful man, who is the bishop's son, came down to the General Conference in Nashville, was examined and ordained, and the presiding bishop sent him out here to Good-loets last November. We don't know anything about him except that he has been fighting in the trenches in France for a year and has had a bullet cut out of his left lung. Everybody adores him, and we all sit spellbound listening to him preach, I think mostly on account of his voice, because none of us ever seems to remember what he is preaching about. He's been having services in the ballroom at the Country Club but he is going to dedicate the chapel soon and we are all relieved. It has been fun to go out to church at the Club twice every Sunday and to prayer meeting on Wednesday night all winter, and we've danced in the long parlor at home and in the double parlors at Jessie Litton's so as not to disarrange the pews, I mean the chairs, in the ballroom, but now that the spring has come we - we need the Club. I'm glad you will be here for the dedication, and you will help us kind of - kind of -"

"Taper off from your religious spree?" I asked with a laugh that Letitia echoed shamefacedly.

"That's an awful way to put it - but -"

"True?"

"We've all tried hard, but - but it is such a - a bore. It doesn't seem fair to enjoy Gregory Goodloe so much at dinners and parties and not show our respect and - and admiration by being good church members. Jessie joined his study workers and she took a class of the awful little children from down in the Settlement beyond the Phosphate Mills, who all smelled terribly. She worked hard with them twice a week for a month, and then Mother Spurlock, who is the front pillar of his congregation, found that she had taught all the dirty little things to sew with their left hands. She came in one morning and found them all stitching away industriously backwards, just because Jessie is left-handed herself. Mother Elsie laughed until she lost her breath and Mr. Goodloe had to help unloosen her belt for her. The meeting broke up with ice cream on Jessie for everybody. We all belong to home mission societies and sewing circles and -"

"You want me to get you out of your purgatory and let you

backslide to -"

"Don't say it!" exclaimed Letitia with a laugh. "But we just want not to hurt his feelings and -"

"We won't," I said grimly. "Now let's talk about the ball out at the Club we are going to give Nickols when he comes down the first of May."

"That's just what I mean. I knew you'd understand and I am so relieved that you are not angry about the chapel and things. We can leave it all to you and we'll have the times of our lives. Billy Harvey says his ankles are getting stiff, it's been so long since he has fox-trotted. Do call Mammy or Sallie and let's look at your clothes." With which Letitia descended from her spiritual heights into the realm of the material and plunged with both Mammy and Sallie into a riot of clothes.

For an hour or two I lay back in my pillows and watched the two black women and the white one indulge in primitive decorative orgies, and from their delight my eyes would glance out and fix themselves wistfully on the dim line of Paradise Ridge which was cut by the square steeple of weathered stone just where Old Harpeth humps itself up above the rest of the Ridge; and something sore and angry and trapped hurt under my breast.

"The earth is the Lord's -" chanted itself in my mind to the tune of "Drink to me only," and my hand curled around the letter under my pillow as if for comfort and - defense.

"It is just as you told me that night at the piano, Nickols dear: 'Religion is the most potent form of intoxication known to the human race,' and apparently all my friends have been getting the drink habit badly. I'll rescue the poor dears and have an interesting time doing it," I said to myself after Letitia had departed with my most choice millinery creation fastened down upon her sleek braids because she found she could not live without it.

And then a strange thing happened, as I lay prone between the lavender-scented sheets spread on the four-poster bed of my foremothers, ready to drift off into another "bone resting" nap. The flood of tears that had risen from my heart when I had sat that night a week ago and listened to that remarkable little baseball evangelist, the tide of which had been rolled back when Nickols had bent his beautiful dark head against mine in Aunt Clara's music room and whispered above the roar of New York, "religion is the most potent form of intoxication" to me, again welled from my heart and this time flooded my lashes and my cheek and my pillow. What was strangest of all, they seemed to wash away all the tears of anger and fear that I had been pressing back into my depths from breakfast time, and left me weak and again ready for sleep. And like a comforted little child, I slept.

It was sunset when I awoke, and I felt as strong as two women and ready for action, the call for which was upon me by the time Sallie had put me into her favorite creation, selected from the ones she had hung in closets and wardrobe.

"Mister Billy Harvey and Mister Hampton Dibrell is down on the front porch ready to gallivant you, honey-bunch, and I seen Miss Letitia and her Mister Cliff Gray coming in one direction and Miss Jessie in another, so I reckon Sallie had better hurry with that New York twilight she's fixing on you," Mammy announced as she stood in my doorway and beamed upon me. "An' I expects the parson will be stepping over likewise fer a few words, seeing you was so sweet and showed sich pretty manners to him this morning," she added with reverent delight.

"Sweet? Showed such pretty manners?" I gasped, as Sallie fastened the last hook and eye and stood beside Mammy to admire me.

"'Twas no more than you oughter done to the preacher, and I was proud of my raising of you when you helt on to him and begged him to stay to dinner. I was sho' disappointed that he had to leave us. I'm a Colored Methodist, I am, and if I do say it, I knows how to shake a young pullet in the skillet fer a preacher's taste, black or white. Now go on down and stop that buzzing fer you on the front porch. Sallie, come and carry out the tea and cakes to the guests," with which command to both of us Mammy rolled her two hundred and fifty pounds down the hall with great majesty, while Sallie meekly followed in her wake.

"Sweet! Showed such pretty manners!" I quoted to myself as I slowly descended the steps and went out on the wide porch to find my friends assembled under the budding rose vine that wreathed the tall white pillars of the Poplars.

The parson was not there.

"Rescued!" exclaimed Billy as he grasped one of my hands and hung on with a very good imitation of a drowning man seizing a lifeline. They all laughed and Hampton Dibrell held my other hand as ardently, though not in quite such light vein. I had to rescue it to accept Clifton Gray's nosegay of huge violets from his greenhouse, and I embraced Jessie with the nosegay pressed to her pink cheeks.

"Oh, Charlotte, I could fox-trot with you a week and not hesitate," exclaimed Billy, still clinging to me.

"Let's begin to-night," I assented warmly. Billy is contagious and to dance with him is a high art.

"Let's motor out to the Club in Hamp's car and mine, have a chicken supper and dance until sun-up," suggested Billy.

"We can stop by and get Mark Morgan and Nell, and I believe Harriet Henderson will come along, if everybody asks her - all the men, I mean," Letitia added with enthusiasm to match Billy's. Harriet Henderson is the latest emerged widow in Goodloets and consequently is most interesting to the masculine world at present.

"Let's start now, so as to give the chicken plenty of time to get into the frying pan and over the fire," said Hampton, who is always the practical member to bring up the details of any situation.

"I'm just from the tennis courts and I'll have to stop to dress, I'm afraid," said Letitia meekly, as if she felt sure of a storm of remonstrance.

"People don't dress to dance these days, Letitia," said Billy, with the greatest innocence of mien and expression, a manner he always uses in speaking to Letitia's rather literal directness and in which he delights greatly. "They undress. You are unclothed enough as to ankles and if you roll the sleeves of your tennis shirt to your shoulders, take off your collar and tuck in the flaps, it will be enough to satisfy our cravings for fashionable and suitable attire. We really want fried chicken rather than chicken -"

"That will do, Billy," Letitia answered him with gentle firmness.

"That was just what I remarked, Letitia dear. That will do, for we want chicken dressed with cream gravy and don't care about any swathed in chiffon. And furthermore -"

"Do hush, Billy; look who's coming," Jessie interrupted him, and there before my eyes I saw my entire group of friends begin to preen themselves into new beings. Letitia smoothed down her skirts a fraction of an inch, rolled down her sleeves another fraction and pushed back into her braids a brown lock that was rioting across her brow. Jessie shook out her muslin ruffles, reefed a fold of net higher across her neck, and pinned it in place with a jeweled pin, while Hampton's and Billy's and Cliff's expressions and poses of countenance and bodies suddenly fell into lines of decorum.

"Great Smokes! We all forgot it was prayer meeting to-night, and it'll be no trotting the fox for ours," Billy groaned, while he rose to his feet with a smile of angelic sweetness. "Hello, Parson! We were just beginning to think about you," was his greeting to the Sacred Jaguar who had come through the garden and around the house. I felt sure that he had heard Billy's plaint of disappointment about the dance, for there was a quick glint of the amethysts as he halted and stood on the walk below us and smiled up at us.

"I welcomed Miss Powers for breakfast, and now I find I want to come over and do it again for tea," he said, and as I was perfectly cool, sober and in my right mind at the moment he spoke, I had to concede that his voice was the most wonderful I had ever heard, and something in me made me resent it as well as the curious veneer that had spread over my friends at his entry upon the scene. There they stood and sat, six perfectly rational, fairly moral, representative free and equal citizens, cowed by the representative of something that they neither understood nor cared about, and it made me furious. They all wanted to go to the Club to dance, to do the natural, usual, perfectly harmless thing, and they were being constrained. If they had wanted to go to the prayer meeting as they wanted to dance, they would have been natural and joyful and eager about it.

"I resent, even *I* resent people's being bored with the God they think exists, and I think it is disrespectful to go into His presence like that," I said to myself, and then I suddenly determined to begin my rescue work for the religiously involved, and now I felt was the appointed time. Also I felt the excitement that comes from turning and facing the foe which has pursued.

"I'm glad you came over, Mr. Goodloe," I said with nice, cool friendliness in my voice. "Billy was just planning a glorious fox-trot for this evening and then suddenly remembered with dismay that you were to have your - entertainment at the Club to-night. Couldn't we - we make some sort of compromise? Or at least couldn't you cut your - prayers short so he can get in an hour or two of his favorite pleasure after - after duty well done?" As I spoke I had come to the edge of the steps and thus stood alone above him, looking down on him with a kind of cool aloofness as if he belonged to another world, while I heard all of his recent converts grouped back of me give little gasps of dismay.

CHAPTER III

THE GAUNTLET

Was that young Methodist minister crushed by my plainly intended gauntlet flung down to him? He was not.

"I'm glad I came over in time to put Billy out of his misery," he answered, smiling up at me with a quick comprehension that was enraging. "I'm going to have informal services in the chapel to-night to try out the acoustics before the contractor turns over the building. I am not satisfied about the sounding board he has put in, and the only way is to try it with at least part of the seats occupied. We'll sing a bit and plan the dedication; not have a formal service. So then, Billy, you can have your fox-trotting and a good time to all of you, bless you, my children." As he spoke he smiled at the entire group with the most delightful interest and pleasure. He was dressed in a straight black coat with a plain silk vest cut around a white collar that buttoned in the back, and his dull gold mane was brushed down sleek and close to his beautiful head. Not a flash of expression in his strong face showed that he felt any resentment or dismay at thus having some of his most prominent church members backslide from his prayer meeting into a fox-trot, and yet I knew - knew that he fully appreciated the situation and laid the blame of it where the blame was due.

"Of course we will come to the services first - that is, if you - if you don't object," Letitia said with her usual directness and lack of any kind of finesse, thus bringing the situation to a decided head.

"Why not come over for the songs and then not stay for the conference?" was the genial answer that positively astonished me, and as he spoke he came up the steps and stood beside me. "Dabney and I found the first Star of Bethlehem when we were weeding this afternoon. I brought it to you carefully, and can I have a cup of that tea he has been trying to make you serve for the last five minutes?" With these words the Reverend Mr. Goodloe turned me around and sent me to the tea tray that Dabney and Sallie had put on a table under the rose vine; but not before he had taken up my hand, put the star flower in it and curled my fingers over it. "I'll pass the muffins, Billy, and you take the cakes for Miss Powers, and be more careful than you were last Sunday with my collection plate for the poor." Billy feigned confusion, accepted the plate and was just about to begin a defense, when a diversion occurred to stop him.

"There comes Mark and Mrs. Mark," he exclaimed, "but they have got an offspring apiece in their embrace and several trailers. Somebody ought to remonstrate with Nell Morgan or have the firmness to apply the superfluous blind kitten treatment every spring. Three children are patriotic, but five are populistic and ought to be frowned upon," and Billy grumbled all the while the Morgans were flocking up the front walk. When they came to the steps the Jaguar descended and held out his clerically befrocked arms so that the gurgler from Mark's shoulder and the giggler from Nell's arms both fell into his embrace at one time. "You young marplots, you!" he said as the gurgler printed a wet kiss on his left ear and regarded him with rapture while the small cooer, proclaimed as feminine by neck and sleeve ribbons, cuddled against his shoulder with soft confidence. "They're going to take you both down to the river and drown you," he confided with a soft note in his voice that was an answer to the coo.

"I wish you would," said Mark, as, with a laugh, he shook my hand extended from the group around me, composed of Nell and the other three kiddies, all crowded together in one passionate greeting. "Nurse and Julia and the house and garden man have all gone to a wedding, so we have fed 'em and are now starting out for a razoo, and we don't care whether it lasts until midnight or not. Young Charlotte, you hug one side of your Aunt Charlotte and let Jimmy get his innings on the other side. Here, break away, all of you!" and while everybody laughed, Mark disentangled the greetings, and seated the separated juvenile members in a row on the steps beside the parson and the two babes. Nell he left in the hollow of my arm.

"Oh, it is so good to have you at home, Charlotte," she said, with another hug. "We miss you terribly. We depend on you for everything. Things don't go right without you. I had a terrible time with - that is, you haven't seen baby yet. Give her to me, Mr. Goodloe," and as she spoke Nell leaned over to get the cooer out of the Jaguar's arms for my inspection.

"You'll get neither Babe nor Suckling," was his answer as he cuddled the two closer and hunched his shoulders in Nell's direction. "Don't you know enough to let well enough alone? If they have got to go out to the Club and fox-trot until midnight they ought to have repose now."

"We promised to be good at church, but we didn't promise anything about the Country Club, and if we go there we are going to be as bad as anybody out there is," announced small Charlotte with determined composure. "Dabney says that fox-trotting is a devil's dance and we want to see you all do it with him."

"Help!" exclaimed Billy, while Mr. Goodloe put his arm around Charlotte and drew her to him with a kind of fierce tenderness.

"Isn't she awful?" exclaimed Nell. "We meant to ask you if we could take them with us out to the Club to prayer meeting. Some of the Settlement women bring their babies and I know mine will be as good. Charlotte and Sue and Jimmy promised, and the sound of your voice bewitches the babies as it does all of us."

As Nell finished speaking and bent to pat the head of the Suckling on his shoulder, the Reverend Mr. Goodloe looked straight into my eyes and laughed, perfect comprehension of me and my revolt in his direct amethyst glances which shot into my depths.

"They are all going over to listen to Mr. Goodloe sing hymns at his chapel, Nell, and then all of you are coming by here for me to go out to the Club to dance a few hours," was my answer to the shot as I calmly refused the invitation into the fold that had been given me with the rest of the backsliding flock.

"We can't go - the babies would never in the world -" Nell was beginning to exclaim.

"Drat 'em!" exclaimed Billy, looking down aggrievedly at the small crew of marplots. "A pair of perfectly good chaperons are hard to get, and to think of that bunch of little miseries getting in the way of a good old fox -"

"They'll all go to sleep during the services and I'll keep them on my bed in the parsonage until the fun is over, and agree to deliver them on claim," Mr. Goodloe interrupted Billy to say with quiet decision.

"Now that is what I call some church relation, nursery and parsonage combined," said Billy with the deepest gratitude. "The rest of you hurry over those muffins, even if you haven't had any of Mammy's for six months, and, since the chicken fry is off, go home to get suppers and ready for psalm-singing and foxing. Parson, you are some sport, and I'll hold both of those puppies while you drink your tea from the hands of fair Charlotte."

"Thank you, I don't believe I want any tea after all, and I think I'll take these 'puppies' on home with me through the garden, for they are both dying to the world." As he spoke the parson rose to his feet and stood with the two drowsing babies in his arms, looking down at me as I stood with his cup of tea in my hand. And as he looked I felt my whole rebellious heart and mind laid bare and I knew that he knew that I was ready to fight him to the last ditch in the battle for possession of the souls of my friends. I would fight for their independence of thought and sincerity of life, and he would fight to lead them off into a far country in quest of what I considered a tradition, a shibboleth, "a potent agent for intoxication" of the reason by which man must progress. I also knew that I faced a foe versed in the warfare between religion and modern scientific decisions about it and that he would be one worthy of my metal. His refusal of my cup of tea, for which he had announced that he came, was his gauntlet and I accepted it as I turned with the queer sugared rage in my heart and set the cup on the table.

And as I had planned, and the Jaguar directed, the evening came to pass. While I slipped into some dancing fluff, the strains of the most wonderful hymn that the Christian religion possesses floated across my garden and into my window and again beat against my heart. The parson was singing with the rest of them, but his voice seemed to lift theirs and bear them aloft on the strong, wide wings that went soaring away into the night, even up to the bright stars that gleamed beyond the tips of the old graybeard poplars. A queer tight breath gripped my heart for a second as his plea, "Abide with me, fast falls the eventide," beat against it, then I laughed it away.

"It *is* 'a potent agent for intoxication' when brewed by the Reverend Mr. Goodloe, and here's where I run, both physically and mentally," I said to myself as I ran down the steps and out to the two cars that stood honking impatiently by the gate.

I don't think I ever enjoyed a dance more, and I am sure that my pleasure was partly due to the wild spirits of the religiously released who were having the first joy fling for six months.

"I'll not get enough until I wilt upon the floor and have to be carried out," said Billy, as he held me closer and slid two steps to the right and then back to get me out of the way of Hampton and Harriet Henderson, who were dancing with regardless joy.

"Will you feel that way about church next Sunday?" I asked him, but my demand made no apparent dent, for he danced on without answering.

At an hour after that of midnight the revelers came home and left me at my gate, by request, to walk alone in the brilliant spring moonlight through my garden to the wide door back of the white pillars. After they had seen me safely started, they glided away and I stood on the steps and watched Nell and Mark reclaim their family from a tall dark figure that carried out two loads to the parental arms. Then the hush that comes upon the world in the midnight hours fell over the Poplars and I stood leaning against one of the tall pillars and reveled in it.

Goodloets is one of the tradition-grayed old towns that are rooted deep in the Harpeth Valley since the days of the Colonies, and in it can be found perhaps the purest Americanism on the American continent. The Poplars, under whose broad roof I made the seventh generation nested and fledged, spreads out its wings and gables upon a low hill which is the first swell of the Harpeth hills, and the rest of the old town stretches out on the hillside before it down to the valley, in which runs the Harpeth River, curving around the town and flowing out of the valley to the Mississippi. Behind the Poplars roll the fields and meadows of the Home Farm, which has given food and sustenance to the Poplars' brood since the days of the redskins, when it was cleared by the first Powers and his servants, with muskets ready to fire into the surrounding forests. To the left of the Poplars and beyond the chapel lies the Settlement, in which those lacking in worldly goods have lived for generations in a kind of semi-poverty, which is about the only poverty known in the Harpeth Valley. Lately, the Settlement has taken unto itself a measure of prosperity, because of the great tannery and harness works in its midst on the banks of the river, which is bringing in gold from Russia and France. Everybody has made money in the last few years, and the fashionable wing of Goodloets to the left of the Poplars shows improvements and restorations that are both costly and sometimes amazing. However, fortunately the inhabitants of the old village are conservative, and very little of the delicious moss of tradition has been scratched off; it has only been clipped into prosperous decorum, and antiquity still flings its glamour over the town.

"I feel as much rooted as one of the old poplars," I said to myself as some whim made me go down the steps and out into the garden, along the walks with their budding borders of narcissus and peonies, down through Nickols' sunken garden to the two oldest of all the poplars that now seemed to be standing sentinel to prevent any raid from me on the little stone meeting house over the lilac hedge. "You dear old graybeard," I said to the one on my left, as I looked up and saw a faint feathering of silver on its branches. And as I spoke I took the old trunk into my embrace and laid my cheek against the rough bark.

And then something happened. Afterwards I was glad that I was leaning against the strength of the old graybeard poplar and hidden behind it.

Suddenly from out the shadows beyond the lilac hedge, through whose bare branches any movement in the yard of the chapel showed plainly, a woman came stumbling along towards the gate and beside her walked the parson with his arm supporting hers. She was sobbing the hard, dry sobs that any woman knows are those of despair, and which call any other woman who hears them. My first impulse was to run to the hedge and speak to her; then I stopped, for I was arrested by what the parson was saying to her.

"What does it matter, Martha? You have your Master's forgiveness and His permission to go and sin no more, even though those sins be as scarlet." And as he spoke his voice was that of quiet authority as if he felt fully his apostolic right to unloose sins upon this earth.

"He'll come back now that *she* has, and he'll come to me again. I can't fight him. I'll slip back into hell. Just give me the money to go out into the city and I'll not bother anybody any more. I'll take the child and I'll die for all anybody in Goodloets ever knows. Lend me the money; I'll send it back!" The girl's voice was hard and defiant and she turned and faced the minister as if at bay. "Give me that money, if all that praying and singing and preaching that you've done is true. I want to go in the morning before he follows her here and puts me in hell again. God won't clean me twice."

"You shall go," came the calm answer in the apostle's beautiful voice, "but I will have to have a few days to provide a place of safety for you in the city, where the child can be cared for while you get suitable work."

"I won't wait. He'll follow her and he'll look down on me and the child and damn me again. I won't wait. I'm weak and I dasn't. Give me that money to-night!" And the demand was passionate and savage.

"Then I'll meet you at the morning train with it and rush you to a place of safety if there is no other way. You must go back home now, and it will be best not to tell anyone where you are going until you no longer fear your weakness, for they might betray your hiding place. Strength will be given you, Martha, if you only ask."

"I'll pray, Parson, I'll pray, now that you are going to give me my chance to get strong enough to be good. I'll work and I'll pray, but hide me until I do get strong." And the hard, dry sobs melted as the girl put her head down upon the gate a moment and then went out through it.

Maria Thompson Daviess

"God bless you, child, and keep you ever in thought of Him," were the words that she carried away with her as she hurried down the street toward the Settlement.

Then for a second some awful fear came across my heart that I did not understand. I now know that it was a premonition of what was to wring my own heart and I cowered against the old tree in agony. Gregory Goodloe was not more than six feet away from me on the other side of the budding, fragrant hedge, and in the moonlight I could see the beautiful strength of his golden head and strong placid face, on which lines of pain were drawn, and I had to restrain myself from crying out to him in my own pain. I wanted to go quickly and cling to his strength. Then I stopped and listened.

He had raised his face to the stars and was praying.

"O Father," he asked, as if speaking to someone with whom he walked in the cool of the midnight, "help the weak on whom the strong prey."

Then he went into the dark door of the little chapel and left me out in the cold midnight alone. The fear was gone, and comforted I went back through my budding garden and arrived at the front door just as old Mr. Pate, the telegraph operator at the little station down the street, turned in at the gate.

"Miss Charlotte," he puffed, as he fairly flung the telegram at me, "this come fer you at ten o'clock and I risked it and run up here with it after I heard them ottermobiles go by. I'm courting Mrs. Jennie Hicks myself and I understands about courtings." And before I could speak he had run on back down the street.

As I stood and looked at the yellow envelope fear again gripped my heart, and without opening it I walked into the house, locking the great door behind me with trembling fingers, and went toward a light I saw shining from the trellised back porch and which I did not understand. I have never in my life been the least bit afraid of anything, except something within my own body, from the hideous pain of my green-apple days to the pain I had felt as I talked beside the piano with Nickols in New York, a thousand miles away; but something made me pause just for a second in the pantry doorway before I stepped into the light upon the porch. I shall never forget the scene that was enacted before my wondering eyes in the dim light of a candle burning upon a table near the refrigerator.

Father stood with a bowl of ice in his hand and his fingers were just closing around a squat, black bottle that I knew contained the rarest and choicest whiskey ever run from a distillery. His iron-gray hair was rampant, his dressing gown fell away from his throat and showed the knotting of the great cords that ran down into his shoulders, and his dark eyes glittered under their heavy, black brows, while his mouth was twisted and white. Then, as I looked, something happened. A stealthy padding of feet came around the house from the garden and up the back steps, under the budding rose vine that was climbing through the trellis as if to clutch at the light, and a huge figure loomed up from out the shadow.

It was the powerful Harpeth Jaguar out hunting, and his weapon was a hoe, while under his arm he carried a roll that looked like a contribution to a rag man of bedding and old clothes.

"I tell you, Mr. Powers, there is frost in the air and I have collected everything in the parsonage that would cover those late anemones. I saw your light and I thought you might add to the collection. Now what would we do if they should be wilted by the frost just as they are ready to burst bud? Our honor is involved with Graveson, who brought the seeds all the way from Guernsey through the trenches of France and trusted them to me for propagation. Why, they represent a man's life work, and that life may be put out by a bullet any moment! We'll have to rescue them." As he spoke, the great jeweled eyes shone with excitement under the dull gold brows and he seemed not to see at all the incriminating ice and bottle.

"Could you get into Mrs. Dabney's linen closet? We've got to have something." He shivered in a little wind that blew under the rose vine with a frosty gust. I was just observing that he was attired in his pajama jacket and gray flannel trousers, and that his bare heels and ankles declared themselves above and at the back of his slippers, when my eyes were drawn to my father's face and rested there. My heart stood still while I watched it change. All the pain and appetite, straining as a beast strains at a leash, faded from his face. The deathly pallor vanished and the color of human blood returned. The glitter in his deep old eyes changed in a second from that of ferocity to that of anxious excitement.

"I do not know where the household linen is kept and I hesitate to disturb Dabney, as he retired with an aching tooth; but I observed a box of my daughter's apparel beside a trunk in the back hall which Dabney had not carried up on account of its weight and which he was requiring his wife to unpack piece by piece. I'll raid it for enough to save our treasures and accept whatever is my just chastisement in the morning," he said in a voice of guilty stealth.

And there I stood in the shadow of the pantry and saw my father take two armfuls of my costly linen and lace out into the garden. Nothing was spared me, for from the window I could see him and the marauding Jaguar weight their perfumed whiteness down with sticks and stones and clods of earth. I suffered, but silently.

"Good night, sir. God's blessing," I heard the rich voice calling as the half-bare feet padded away as swiftly as they had come through the garden, leaving father standing under the rose vine watching him go. And I watched father - and for some reason my breath seemed suspended in my lungs.

For a very long minute he stood looking at the ice bowl and the bottle; then with a queer wry smile he walked over and put them both in the refrigerator, though the bottle's place was in the sideboard, and closed the door carefully. Then he paused again and said under his breath, "*You*, Judge Nickols Morris Powers!" He smiled at himself with humorous pity and tiptoed past me into the front hall and up the stairway to his rooms above.

I seemed to feel strange padding footsteps down in my depths and I also tiptoed up to my room after I had heard his door shut.

After I had switched on my light (for under the roof of the Poplars electricity had come to aid the candles of hallowed tradition, and was called by Mammy, in deep suspicion, "ha'nt light") I discovered clutched in my cold fingers the yellow envelope the romantic Mr. Pate had brought to me in the midnight. It read:

> "Am coming down on Friday. Am afraid to trust the world and the flesh and think the third member of the carnal firm ought to be on the job.   N."

"Now I am frightened really," I confided to myself as I slipped between the scented sheets and drew a corner of the rose-colored blanket over my head. "I don't know what to do."

Maria Thompson Daviess

CHAPTER IV

TO TURKEY GULCH

The next morning I was very late in descending to my breakfast, but arrived in time to witness Mammy's arraignment of my father, which was conducted in perfect respect, but with great severity.

"I know, Jedge, that menfolks don't know lace that costs a million dollars a yard from a blind woman's tatting, and that's what makes me say what I does, that it sure am dangersome fer 'em to go on a rampage in womenfolks' trunks. I ain't never goin' to git the stains from them clods of earth outen my lambs' clothes, even if the minister did help you put 'em on 'em."

"But, Melissa, those anemones were more valuable than any lace ever manufactured, and I am sure that Charlotte will absolve me when she hears of the exigencies of the case," father pleaded over the top of his morning paper. Mammy was pretending to dust his study, as a blind to the lecture she was administering.

"Yes, sir, I knows all that; but that lace was a heap more valuable than that toothache in that wuthless Dabney's jaw, which he could er wropped up, and hunted out all the old sheets for you instid of that petticoat with them real lace ruffles," was Mammy's firm rejoinder, while she passed a feather duster over the table and rolled her eyes at Dabney.

"Let's let them both off this time, Mammy. Dabney can take the trunks where they belong and lock them up," I said, as I went toward the dining room, while she followed to minister upon my tardiness.

"Them was all your finest lingerings," she said as she plied me with breakfast. "And they was all lost on menfolks. They hasn't even one lady rode by while I had 'em on the line in the sunshine," she grumbled as she finally retired to the kitchen.

After finishing my coffee I sauntered to the front of the house, led by a chorus of hearty laughter in a fluty tenor voice, accompanied by a bass growl, in which I was sure that father was recounting the scrape in which his and the Reverend Mr. Goodloe's anemone adventure had got them. I assured myself that I was annoyed by this repeated early morning invasion of ministerial calls and intended to retire to my room until it was over, but without knowing why, I found myself in the library and greeting the enemy.

"Please forgive us. The case was one of dire necessity," the Reverend Mr. Goodloe pleaded, as he rose and took my hand in his, and held it in such a way that I was forced to look in his face and smile, whether I wished it or not.

"From ambush I saw you take them, and I was powerless to prevent," I answered with a smile at father.

"I came over to ask you if you wouldn't like to go away out into the Harpeth Hills on a mission with me this wonderful morning. I don't know exactly whether I am called to officiate at a birth or a death or that intermediate festivity, a wedding. This is the summons from an old friend of mine:" As he spoke he held out to me a greasy paper on which were a few words scrawled with a pencil.

"Parson we need you in the morning bad. Please come with Bill as brings this. Bring a bible and liniment and oblige your true friend Jed Bangs and wife."

"Isn't your friend Bill able to elucidate?" I asked, as I passed the paper on to father.

"Bill seems to be dumb without being deaf and has no histrionic talent to act out the necessity, so I'm going with him. The Bangs family live up on old Harpeth at Turkey Gulch, and Jed has shot partridges with me all winter. Please, you and the Judge, come with me. I can get the car over Paradise Ridge if I turn it into a wildcat. The morning is delicious, and I feel that I'll need you both." Never in the world have I heard a man's voice with such compelling notes in it that range from a soft coax to a quiet command.

I had not the slightest idea of going with him and I was about to refuse with as much sugary hauteur as I dared use to him, when I looked into father's face and accepted. I had never been on a picnic with my father in my life and I could not understand the pleading in his eyes for my acceptance of this invitation to an adventure in his company, but then, several times since I had come home, I had seen a father I had never known before, and he fascinated me.

"The mountain laurel is in bloom and the rhododendron, and you are a very gracious lady," the Reverend Mr. Goodloe assured me with a deep bow over my hand, which he kissed in a very delightful foreign fashion which made Mammy, who had come to the door to hear my decision, roll her eyes in astonishment which, however, held no hint of criticism, for with her the spiritual king could do no wrong.

"I got a snack fixed up jest's soon as that Dabney tol' me about the junket," she announced. "And I'll put a little wine jelly and flannels in if it am a baby and a bunch of white jessimings in case it am a death."

"Suppose it is a wedding?" I asked her.

"I don't take no notice of weddings. It was a wedding that got me into all the trouble of that Dabney and his wuthless son,

Jefferson, what ain't like me in no way." With which fling at Dabney - who was hovering at the door - she rolled herself back to her kitchen.

"What have you been doing to her now, you rascal?" father demanded of Dabney, who was handing him his hat and holding out his light overcoat to put him into it.

"I jist stepped into the kitchen while her light rolls fer supper was raisin' and got a ruckus fer it," was his mild answer. Dabney lived his connubial life mildly in the midst of the storms of his better half.

"Well, don't do it again. And put that spade in Mr. Goodloe's car, for I'm going to bring in some honeysuckle roots and a laurel sprout or two to try out in the garden," father commanded, as I took my coat and hat from the chair where I had thrown them the afternoon before, and went out to the very unministerial-looking car which stood before the parsonage.

Of course, I had accepted the Reverend Mr. Goodloe's invitation for the journey out into the hills in order to sit beside this very new kind of father I was dimly discovering myself to possess, but I do not to this day know how it happened that I was crushed against the arm steering the gray racer as we sped through Goodloets toward Old Harpeth, while the judge sat beaming, though silent, beside the more silent Bill - who did not beam, but looked out at the road ahead with the shadow in his face of the fatalism that so many of the mountain folk possess.

We were just turning out from the edge of the town, past the last house with its stately white pillars, when a bunch of pink-and-white precipitated itself directly in front of the car - which made the first of the wildcat springs that its master had prophesied for it and then stood with its engine palpitating with what seemed like mechanical fear, while I buried my head on the strong arm next to me, which I could feel tremble for an instant as the Reverend Mr. Goodloe breathed a fervent, "Thank God." Father rose from his seat with a good round oath and silent Bill snorted like a wild animal.

"Why didn't you stop when you saw me coming?" an imperious young voice demanded in tones of distinct anger, and Charlotte, my name daughter of the house of Morgan, calmly climbed up on the running board, over the door next to father, and settled herself in between him and the silent Bill. "Now you can go on," she calmly announced, in a very much mollified tone of voice as she shook out her ruffles into a less compressed state and wiped her face with her dirty hand, much to the detriment of the roses in her cheeks.

"Where are you going, Charlotte, may I inquire?" asked the Reverend Mr. Goodloe in a cheerful and calm voice, though I saw that his fingers still trembled on the steering wheel as he held back the enraged gray engine. I was still speechless and I saw that father was in the same condition.

"You said I might go 'next time' when my Auntie Harriet didn't want me to go with you last Tuesday on account of my stomach from the raw potato Jimmy dared me to eat. This is that time," she calmly answered, as she gave an interested look at the silent Bill and again settled the short, pink skirts.

"Yes, I did say that," admitted Mr. Goodloe, as he turned in his seat as far as he could and began to argue the question. "But we shall be gone almost all day and I am afraid your mother wouldn't want you to be gone that long."

"Is it true for you to say that when you know that she will be mighty glad for you to keep me safe with you all day?" Charlotte demanded of him, looking directly into his smiling, friendly face.

"No, that wasn't quite honest, I'll admit," he answered her gravely with the guilt of conviction showing in his face just as plainly as it would have shown if one of his deacons had caught him evading a question of grave moment. "And as it is the fulfillment of a promise which you claim, I am going to ask Miss Powers and the judge if they will permit me to add you to the party, and then go and get permission from your mother to take you with us."

"My mother told me to go and bother Auntie Charlotte an hour or two and that was when I met you. I ran into the car just minding my mother," Charlotte answered him with calm pride at her near achievement of death through literal obedience.

"Just drive by and we'll call to Nell. I am afraid the case must have been desperate, for I am seldom the victim," I said in an undertone to our host, who acquiesced with a laugh. "Harriet Henderson must be dead, for Nell usually sends the worse one to her," I added under my breath.

"My Auntie Harriet is having a man cut the ache out of one of her teeth," Charlotte remarked, apropos of nothing, as the huge car swung around into the street in which the Morgans reside. "And, besides, I don't like her any more, because, when she said Sue had to have part of the doll house she bought for us to play in down at her home, and I said then Sue would have to take the outside because I wanted the inside, she locked it up for all this week."

"The modern business acumen of the feministic persuasion," father remarked, as we all laughed at this candid revelation of an egocentric attitude of mind in small Charlotte.

After a few whirls of the gray wheels we paused a moment at the Morgan gate.

"Heavens, yes, and thank you," called Nell in response to our demand for her small daughter's company. "If I had another one clean, I'd give it to you."

"Better go on quick, for Jimmy can wash in a piece of a minute if he wants to," warned Charlotte, and in a second the parson had sent the gray car flying out toward Old Harpeth, though I saw him glance back with a trace of distress in his eyes at the fading vision of a small boy running, howling, to the front gate of the Morgan residence.

"Now mother'll whip him for crying if she does as she says she would, but she won't," observed the tender big sister, as she rose to her feet and waved a maddening farewell to the distressed urchin being left behind.

"Is she totally depraved?" I asked of the young Charlotte's spiritual adviser at my side.

"No; perfectly honest," he answered me with a glint in his eyes that was a laughing challenge.

"There is something awful about honesty," I answered, without appearing to notice the glint.

"There wouldn't be if it were a universal custom," was the answer I got as we whirled by a farmer's wood lot and began to climb the first foothill of Old Harpeth.

All my life I have been going out to Old Harpeth on excursions, but never had I spent a day like the one I had begun with the Jaguar in his native fastnesses. The whole old mountain was beginning to bud and I could almost see it draping on a regal Persian garment of rose and green threaded with purple and blue woven against the old brown and gray of the earth color. The wine-colored trillium with its huge spotted leaves, the slender white dog-tooth violets, the rose-pink arbutus, the blue star myrtle and the crimson oak buds, were matted into a vast robe that was gorgeously oriental, while a perfume that was surely more delicious than any ever wafted from the gardens of Arabia floated past us in gusts through which the gray car sped without the slightest shortness of breath. I seemed a million miles away from the great fetid city in which I had been living - and fast going farther. As we wound up and up into the great forest which is the crown of Old Harpeth, we could look down through occasional vistas and see the Harpeth River curling and bending through pastures in which the chocolate plowed fields were laid off in huge checks with the green meadows, while the farmhouses and barns dotted the valley like the crude figures on a hand-woven chintz.

There are very few men who know enough not to talk to a woman when she has no desire for their conversation, but the Reverend Jaguar seemed to be one of the variety who comprehend the value of silences, and neither of us spoke for at least ten miles, though, of course, it was his duty to make hay while the sun of my nature shone upon him and delicately to inquire into my spiritual condition. He didn't. He just let the wind blow into my empty spaces and kept his eyes and thoughts on the road ahead of him. Charlotte's chatter with father was blown back from me and I was happy in a kind of aloneness I had never felt before.

"We are in Hastings County now and in a few minutes we shall be in Hicks Center, the county seat," were the first words that broke in on my self-communion as we began to speed past rough board and log cabins, each surrounded by a picket fence which in no way seemed to fend the doorsteps from razor-back pigs, chickens and a few young mules and calves. "It must be court day, for I don't see a single inhabitant sitting chewing under his own vine and fig tree."

"Yes; it's the first Monday," answered father, as the gray machine pulled gallantly through a few hundred feet of thick, black mud and turned from the wilderness into the public square of the metropolis of Hicks Center.

"Yes, court is in session and there the whole population is in the courthouse," said father, as we glided slowly down the village street. "They must be trying a murder or a horse-stealing case," and I saw his eyes gleam for a second under their heavy brows as the eyes of an old war horse must gleam when he scents powder.

"Ugh," assented silent Bill, making the first remark of the journey, and as he spoke the syllable he rose and pointed to the courthouse, which stood in the midst of a mud-covered public square, completely surrounded by hitching-posts to which were hitched all the vehicles of locomotion of the last century down to the present in Hicks Center - which had not as yet arrived as far as the day of the motor car.

"Is Jed in there, Bill?" demanded the Reverend Mr. Goodloe; and as Bill assented with muscular vigor, if not vocal, he drew the gray car up beside, an old-fashioned carryall, whose wheels were at least five feet high and which had hitched to its pole an old horse and a young mule.

"That team makes a nice balance of - temperament," Mr. Goodloe remarked, as he lifted out Charlotte and then turned to swing me, in his strong arms, free of a mud puddle and onto the old brick pavement which was green with the moss of generations.

Then, piloted by the silent Bill, we made our way through a quiet throng of men and women and children, from the awkward age of shoe-top trousers and skirts to that which, in many cases, was partaking from the maternal fount, as the women stood in groups and whispered as they looked at us shyly. Somehow their decorous calico skirts, which just cleared the ground, made me feel naked in my own of white corduroy, which was all of eight inches from the mud in which theirs had draggled.

And as silent as they, even Charlotte's chatter subdued, we entered the court room and were led through a crowd up to the front seat. At least the rest of us were seated, but the judge, jury and prisoner and prosecuting attorney rose in a body and shook hands with the Reverend Mr. Goodloe as if he were their common and best beloved son.

"He's been in the Harpeth Valley less than a year, and look at that. We've been here all our lives and they don't know who we are," whispered father, with the same pride shining in his eyes that shone upon the parson from the eyes of the gaunt prisoner, who rose and shook hands with Mr. Goodloe with the sheriff beside him, while the rough old judge from the bench waited his turn.

"We accommodated Jed by waiting until you come before we begun his trial, Parson," the judge said, as he turned back to his bench, which was a splint-bottom chair behind a rude table, dignity being lent to the chair by its being the only one in the room. The rest of the population of the court room of Hicks Center were seated upon benches made of split and hewn logs.

"Thank you, Mr. Hilldrop," said the Reverend Mr. Goodloe, as he sat down beside the prisoner and began a whispered conversation with him.

"The court have come to order. Shoot ahead, Jim, and tell us what Jed have done and how he done it," commanded the judge, as he tilted back his chair, took out his knife and began to whittle a stick of bright red cedar. Twelve good men and true, attired in butternut trousers stuffed into muddy boots, settled themselves in the jury box, which was a log bench set at right angles to the other benches, a little apart from the table and chair of the judge, and nine of them took out their knives and bits of cedar and began to follow the lead of the judge in making fine pink curls fall upon the floor.

"May it please your honor, the prisoner is charged with the stealing of a young mule," said a lanky young mountain lawyer, who had put on a coat over his flannel shirt and brushed a little patch of tow hair just above his brows in deference to his position of prosecuting attorney.

"State yo' case," commanded the judge, as he tried the point of his splinter against his thumb to test its whittled sharpness.

Maria Thompson Daviess

"Hiram Turner, over at Sycamore, lent Jed a team of mules to haul his daughter, who married Jed, home in a wagon with her beds and truck, and when he come down Paradise Ridge to git the team, Jed claimed one had got away from him and run off in the big woods. They was a horse and mule trader come along the same day Jed lost the mule and when Hi and his boy, Bud, knocked Jed down in a fight they found fifty dollars on him in a wad what he won't say where he got it."

With which concise statement the prosecuting attorney sat down and fanned his perspiring brow with his ragged felt hat.

"Got anything to say, Jed?" inquired the judge in a friendly and leisurely fashion, after the accused had been duly sworn in by the sheriff. "How come a man like you to let a mule git away from him?"

With the judge's friendly question there entered another actor on the scene, in the person of a mountain girl who had been cowering on a bench just behind Jed, her face hidden by a black calico split bonnet.

"Please lemme tell, Jed," she pleaded in a soft whisper that only father and I heard, as we sat just behind her.

"Naw," was the one word he gave her, but it was spoken with a soft little purr in his husky voice. Then he answered the judge with a kind of quiet dignity, which I saw that the twelve booted jurymen listened to with respect.

"Jedge," he said, with a stern look into the judge's face, "I reckon you'll have to send me down to the pen. I let that mule git away from me and I didn't steal or sell him; that is all I got to say." And he sat down. I felt father start at my side and then sink back onto his bench.

"Where did you git the money, Jed?" the judge demanded.

"That I ain't a-telling," answered Jed determinedly. "Jest send me down to the pen, fer you-all know all you'll ever know."

"Well, Jed," the judge was beginning to say in an argumentative tone of voice, when father arose and stepped in front of the bench.

"May it please your honor to appoint a counsel for the defense?" he asked in a ringing voice that brought all the outsiders crowding into the door. I had never heard or seen my father in a court room and I had never suspected him of the resonant silver voice with which he made his demand.

"We ain't got a lawyer in Hicks Center but Jim Handy here, and he can't prosecute and defend too. I always kinder looks out fer the prisoners myself," answered the judge.

"Then may I offer myself to the prisoner to conduct his defense?" father demanded, and he looked over at Jed, who in turn looked at Mr. Goodloe before he nodded.

"Then shoot ahead, stranger. Jim have told all they is about it, but you can have Hi and Bud Turner sworn in and git any more they have got to say. Them men speaks truth when they speaks." At which statement every good man and true nodded his head with firm conviction. A gaunt old mountaineer who sat over by the window cleared his throat in an embarrassment that marked him as the Hiram Turner alluded to.

"I don't think I shall need the testimony of Mr. Turner or his son," father answered quietly, as he stood tall and straight before the jury. "I want to put Mr. Bangs' wife on the witness stand and question her before the jury. Sheriff, call Mrs. Bangs."

"Naw, stranger, naw," said Jed, and he rose as if to combat, but Mr. Goodloe laid a restraining hand on his arm, and trembling, he took his seat.

"Don't tell nothing, honey," he whispered, as the girl rose

from her bench, laid aside her cavernous black bonnet and advanced, took the oath administered by the sheriff and stood facing father.

"Now, Mrs. Bangs," said father, with silvery tenderness in his voice which I felt sure had gained him the reputation of never having lost a case in which a woman was involved, "I want you to tell us all that happened on the day that Jed let the mule escape him. Look at me and tell me all about it."

"Well, stranger," began the mountain girl, with a look of confidence coming into her face that was like a little pink wide-open arbutus, "I reckon you won't believe me - like Jed didn't at first, though he do now."

"Don't tell, honey," the prisoner commanded and implored in the one plea. "I'd rather take the pen. They won't believe you."

"It war this way," she continued, without seeming to hear the command of her young husband, upon whose arm the parson again laid a restraining hand. "Jed he had unhitched the team and tied them with their rope halters to the fence 'fore our cabin, when it was almost dark 'fore we got thar. Then while I was unpacking the wagon he got on one horse and rid down the side of the gulch to see whar water was at. I was jest takin' the things in when a man come along leading five mules and riding on one. He was a city stranger in fine clothes and he asked me fer a meal because he had lost his way from a man who had a tent and grub. My mammy allus cooked fer strangers, so -"

"She shore do that," ejaculated Mr. Turner, proud of his noted hospitality.

"So I made up a fire hasty in the yard and put on a coffee pot," the girl continued. "I had some corn pone and bacon my mammy had give me fer a snack and I het that up. Whilst I got the meal the stranger he went on unloading our wagon and then he come to a bundle of bed quilts what my mammy have been saving fer me from her mammy and her grandmammy. He took a notion to them and ast me how old they was and I told him about as old as any twenty-inch cedar on Old Harpeth. He asked me to trade 'em, but I couldn't abear to until he had riz to fifty dollars, what was the price of a young mule, all on account of his sister wanting quilts like them up in a big city. I was kinder crying quiet at letting 'em go, but I thought about what that mule would be to Jed who wuz so good to me, so I give 'em to him and he tied 'em on his saddle and went away. It war most a hour when Jed come and when I told him and showed him the money, he didn't believe me about them old quilts and he tooken the rope from around the neck of the mule he'd been riding and -"

She paused here in her story and put her scarlet flower face in her hands, while Jed groaned and dropped his own face down upon his arm. The old judge's face took on a grim sternness, the jury stopped whittling and the face of every woman in the court room gazed upon the girl with stern unbelieving accusation.

"Go on, now, honey, but they won't believe you," commanded Jed with a sob.

"Your husband took the rope from around the neck of the mule and left him untied?" asked father gently.

"What fer, Melissa?" asked the old judge, without gentleness or any show of confidence in what the shrinking woman was saying.

"To beat me with. He war crazed mad and called me a name, but I don't hold it ag'in him," answered the young wife, with a glance at the cowering prisoner.

"He done right," calmly announced one of the twelve good men and true, in the muddy boots and flannel shirt, and every mountain woman in the court room nodded her head in approval of the pronouncement.

"Order in the court room. You all shet up and listen," commanded the judge, as father looked around the room and then at him with a stern demand for control of the situation.

"Then what happened, Mrs. Bangs?" father continued to question.

"I hollered and fought and skeered the mule off into the big woods where he can't be found to keep my husband out of the pen," she answered with a sob. "It took me a week to make him believe about them quilts and then pappy come along and fought him about the mule and found the money, as he claimed he sold the mule fer what was the quilt money."

"That will do. Thank you, Mrs. Bangs," said father, with the same deference and tenderness he had used when he began to question her. "Does the prosecution wish to question the witness?"

"They ain't no use of questioning her when she says a man give her fifty dollars fer five old quilts," was the answer made by the young prosecuting attorney, who did not rise to his feet to make this remark.

"Please ask Mrs. Bangs if the quilts were woven ones of three colors, and then call me to the stand," I said to father quickly.

He put the question to the weeping young wife and got an affirmative answer, after which he dismissed her and had the sheriff swear me in.

"Can you throw any light upon the matter of the purchase or sale of these quilts, Miss Powers?" father questioned me formally.

"If they were old hand-woven, herb-dyed, knitted quilts, they are worth fifty dollars apiece in New York to-day. I paid that for one not five months ago," I said, staring haughtily into the calmly doubting faces of the mountaineers in the jury box and on the benches.

"Do you want to question the witness?" my father asked of the indolent young prosecutor.

"Don't know who she is and don't believe she is telling the truth," was the laconic refusal of the prosecutor to let me influence his case.

"Well, now, Jim, Parson Goodloe here brought the gal along with him and I reckon he can character witness for her," interposed the judge. "Sheriff, swear in the parson." His command was duly executed.

"Mr. Goodloe, do you consider Miss Powers a woman who can be depended upon to speak the truth?" father asked him formally.

"I do," the Reverend Mr. Goodloe answered quietly, and just for a second a gleam from his eyes under their dull gold brows shot across the distance to me, and if it hadn't all been so serious I should have laughed with glee at his thus having to declare himself about my character in public. But the next moment the situation became much more serious and my heart positively stopped still as I seemed to see prison doors close upon the young husband.

"Do you want to question the witness?" father asked of the lolling young prosecutor.

"How long have you known the lady, Parson?" he asked, with a drawl and one eye half closed.

There was an intense silence in the court room for almost a minute. Then the Reverend Mr. Gregory Goodloe answered calmly:

"Three days."

"That might be long enough fer a parson, but it ain't fer a jury," the young attorney answered, and there was a quizzical kindness in the old judge's face as he smiled at Mr. Goodloe and shook his head.

Mr. Goodloe started to speak, but father waved him back to his seat, turned to the judge and jury and began the most wonderful speech on the subject of circumstantial evidence and ethical law that I have ever heard. His beautiful deep voice was as clear as a bell and twenty years seemed to have fallen from his shoulders. I was looking at and listening to the man he had been before I was born. And when I could tear my eyes from his radiant face I watched these stolid mountaineers with whom he was working his will with a power they had never experienced before and did not understand. The men in the jury box and the men on the hewn benches dropped their eyes before his flaming ones as he shamed their censorious manhood and some of the sun-bonneted women bent their heads and sobbed when he arraigned them for the lack of motherhood and sisterhood for the poor young wife who had come over the Ridge to live among them.

"Would you men and women rather believe a girl light of love and faithless, and send your neighbor to prison for two years of his young life when he could mean much to you and his state and his nation, than to give them a little human sympathy and justice. Do you prefer to pin your faith to the value of a worthless, vagrant mule than -"

But just here, when Judge Nickols Morris Powers was winding himself up for one of the greatest appeals to a jury he had ever made, a mule stepped into the case and took away the honor of its winning. He poked his inquisitive nose into a back window of the court room which looked out upon the edge of the big woods, and gave the whole assemblage a hew-haw of derision.

"Lordy mighty, that are Pete come back hisself with all the curkles in the big woods sticking to him!" exclaimed Hiram Turner, as he rose and went to examine his property. "He wasn't sold to no mule man, fer they crops the hair on their hoofs to see if they's healthy 'fore they buys. This here frees Jed."

"And now that you gentlemen have the testimony of a mule, will you not believe the word of Mrs. Bangs and Miss Powers about the valuable quilts?" my father said, after he had commanded silence by raising his hand.

"We shore do believe every word of it, stranger, and you won this here case and not that mule," a stern old sister in a gingham apron and black bonnet said, with a commanding glance at the jury.

"Yes, stranger," answered the hoary old foreman, whom to this day I believe to be the meek husband of the commanding old woman in the black bonnet. "I have done got the mind of the jury and they all voted fer you and not the mule."

"I hereby gives that mule to Jed Bangs and my daughter, Melissa, and I'll knock off a half on the price of his teammate to Jed if he gives me his fergiveness and hern," old Hiram rose and turned with his hand on the forelock of the mule hero to say to the assembled court room. "Go around and halter him quick, Jed, 'fore he breaks away again, the durned fool," he added in another voice.

"Yes, prisoner, you are declared free, and hurry to ketch him, fer he's straining ag'inst Hiram," was the judge's sentence, delivered from the bench as everybody rose and began to stream out to watch the tussle between Jed and the wild mule. Father and the parson were among the first to gain the door.

In the next few minutes I found that some of the shy mountain women were beginning to hover about me, and in another ten minutes I had laid the foundations of an export rug and quilt business that I have a feeling will thrive greatly.

"Were you arrested because your mother told you not to sell

Maria Thompson Daviess

the quilts?" was Charlotte's sympathetic question to the young Mrs. Bangs; and I saw the mite take a clean handkerchief from her small pink pocket and apply it to the tears that were coursing down Melissa's cheeks over the dimples which her smiling mouth was putting in their way. "Just be a good girl and God will forgive you," she comforted further, nestling a dirty pink cheek, which rubbed off, against Melissa's wet one.

"And I asked if she were totally depraved, less than an hour ago," I apologized to my name daughter in my heart.

All the way home I sat beside father, and once I laid a timid hand in his, through whose fingers the pride I had in him must have flowed into his. He flushed for a second and then was pale again.

"You can't put new wine in old bottles, daughter," he said sadly, as he glanced down into the valley. The car was running smoothly, slowly and noiselessly around a sharp curve, and the Reverend Mr. Goodloe both heard and answered the sad axiom.

"The finest wine mellows in casks and is then bottled free of dregs, Judge. I think the wine of life is of that vintage," he said, with one of his radiant smiles that I could see fairly warm father from his paleness.

"I wonder just what he meant by 'the wine of life,'" I asked myself as I went to say good night to Old Harpeth after I put out my light before going to bed.

CHAPTER V

HAVING IT OUT

"Well, of course, we knew Nickols would follow you, Charlotte, but we did hope to have you all to ourselves for more than just a week," moaned Nell Morgan, as we all sat on the front porch of the Poplars in the warm spring sunlight several mornings after I had told them of Nickols' arrival on Friday, which announcement had come in the midnight telegram. I winced at the words "follow you," and then smiled at the absurdity of the little shudder.

"Yes, Nickols will be absorbing, but we can all sit hard on him and perhaps put him in his place," responded Letitia Cockrell, as she drew a fine thread through a ruffle she was making to adorn some part of the person of one of Nell's progeny. "I do not believe in ever allowing a man to take more than his share of a woman's time."

"Do you use grocery scales or a pint cup to measure out Cliff Gray's daily portion of yourself, Letitia?" asked Harriet Henderson, with a very sophisticated laugh in which Nell joined with a little giggle. Harriet was appliqueing velvet violets on a gray chiffon scarf and was doing it with the zest of the newly liberated. Roger Henderson had had a lot of money that, in default of a will, the law gave mostly to Harriet, but in life he had not had the joy of seeing her spend it that he might have had if he could have gazed back from placid death. "Do you make the same allowance of affection to him in the light

Maria Thompson Daviess

of the moon that you do in the dark?" she further demanded of the serene Letitia.

"Well, he doesn't have to see his share divided up into bits and handed out to the other men," was the serene answer to Harriet's gibe and which was pretty good for Letitia.

"My dear child," declaimed Harriet, as she poised a purple violet on the end of her needle, "don't ever, ever make the mistake of letting one of the creatures know just what is coming to him. Isn't that right, Nell?"

"Yes, and it is pretty hard to keep them in a state of uncertainty about you when there are four certain children between you, but I go over to visit my mother at Hillsboro as often as she'll have the caravan and plead with Billy Harvey or Hampton Dibrell to keep me out until I'm late for dinner every time they pick me up for a little charitable spin. That and other deceptions have kept Mark Morgan uncertainly happy so far, but if I am pushed to the wall I'll - I'll go to the Reverend Mr. Goodloe's study for ministerial counsel like you did last Friday afternoon, Harriet," was Nell's contribution to the discussion, which she delivered over the head of the Suckling on her breast.

"Now how did you get hold of that choice bit of scandal, Nellie?" asked Harriet, with serene interest as she bit off a tag of purple silk thread from the stem of one of her violets.

"Billy Harvey says that scandal is a yellow pup that dogs a parson's heels, to which everybody throws some kind of bone," remarked Jessie. Jessie always vigorously represses Billy in his own presence and then quotes him eternally when he is absent.

"Mother Spurlock had come over from the Settlement to see him about the state of the treasury of the Mothers' Aid Class, and she stopped in to get a bundle of clothes I had for her," Nell answered Harriet's question. "She said she didn't mind the hour lost if the parson could give a 'wee bit of comfort' to your 'wrestling' soul. I didn't like to tell her that I thought it might be Mr. Goodloe who was wrestling - for life and liberty - for you and I have been friends since we could toddle, Harriet, but it was temptation to share my anxiety with her." And serenely Nellie patted the back of the drowsing Suckling.

"Wrong this time, Nell," answered Harriet, as she placed still another violet. "I was doing the wrestling, but I went to the mat. I gave up twenty-five dollars and took the directorship of that Mothers' Aid. Never having been a mother, I pointed out to him that I was not exactly qualified, but he laid stress upon my energy and business acumen and I gave up. I mentioned you for the honor, but those marvelous eyes of his glowed with some sort of inner warmth and he said that you had all you could do and would need help from me just as the women at the Settlement do. I'm going to present your Susan with a frock out of that linen and real Valenciennes I bought in the city last week for a blouse for my own self, and I'm going to give the making to that little Burns woman, who sews so beautifully and cheaply to support her seven offspring, while Mr. Burns supports 'The Last Chance' saloon down at the end of the road. In that way I'll be aiding two of Mr. Goodloe's flock at the same time, and when I told him my decision he laughed and said be sure and have it made two inches shorter than you made Sue's frocks, because her bare knees ought not to be hid from the world. That was about all that transpired in the whole hour of spiritual conference you are spreading the scandal about, and you ought to be ashamed."

Suddenly something in me made me determine to have it out with those four women and see what results I could get. I felt thirsty for knowledge of the wellsprings of other people's lives.

"Harriet," I demanded, "just why did you join Mr. Goodloe's church?"

"Let's see," answered Harriet, as she poised a violet and gave herself up to introspection.

"Mr. Goodloe?" I asked squarely, and my honesty drew its spark from hers.

"Mostly," she answered briefly. "And I believe in the church as an institution," she added, with honest justice to herself.

"I think it is absolutely horrid of you to ask a question like that, Charlotte," said Nell, as she turned the fretting Suckling over on her knee and began another series of pats. "We all of us went to church and Sunday school when we were children."

"Up to the time I left, not a single one of you ever had gone to church with any kind of regularity and not a one of you had ever supported its institutions. I've been here less than a week and each one of you has in some way shown me how bored you are with the relation. That's all the case I have against your or any church - just that the members are bored. Also, do any of you get any help in your daily lives, aside from the emotional pleasure it is to you to hear your minister sing twice a week, which would be as great or greater if he sang love and waltz songs from light opera for you?"

And as I asked my question I looked quickly from one to the other of the four women seated with me under the roof of the Poplars and tried to search out what was in their hearts. I knew them and their lives with the cruel completeness it is given to friends to know each other in small towns like Goodloets and I could probe with a certain touch. And as they all sat silent with me, each one driven to self-question by my demand, I threw the flash of a searchlight into each of them. These are some of the things that stood out in the illumination:

Harriet Henderson has always been in love with Mark Morgan, since her shoe-top-dress days, and she married Roger Henderson because Mark was as poor as she before the Phosphate Company gave him his managership. Nell and the babies are the nails driven in her heart every day and she loves them all passionately. She is only twenty-eight and life will be long for her. She needs help to live it. Whence will the help come?

Nell married Mark when she was eighteen and has produced a result every year and a half since. She loves him mildly and he loves her after a fashion, but her endurance is wearing thin. His mother had seven children and he thinks that an ideal number, though she was one generation nearer the pioneer woman and also had a nurse trained in slavery who was a wizard with children. Mark wants to have a lot of joy of life and so far he drags poor exhausted Nell with him. It is a question how long she can stand the social pace and the over-production. What is going to help her when she breaks down? How will she hold him faithful while she rears and trains all the kiddies? Where will she get spirit to love him and work out their salvation? Also Harriet is always there. Something will have to help Nell. What?

Billy loves Nell and doesn't know it. He loved her before she was married. The children make him rage superficially and burn inwardly. He gambles and drinks, but is honest and adorable. What is going to make a real man of him?

Jessie Litton's mother died in a private sanitarium for the mentally unbalanced and she knows all about it. She loves Hampton Dibrell and never looks in his direction or is a moment alone with him. He is in the unattached state of ease where any woman can get him if she cares to try, and Jessie has to keep her hands behind her.

Letitia is serenely happy with not a dark corner that I know of. She loves Cliff Gray and always will. Cliff is faithful and as good as gold, but he will hang around Jessie, who encourages him, because she is lonely and considers him safely tied up with Letitia. Mr. Cockrell is the best lawyer in town and Mrs. Cockrell the most devoted wife and mother. I can only feel that Letitia Cockrell needs a jolt and I don't see where it is coming from.

And I? I am lonely. And I feel that the constant anxiety about father is more than I can bear, worse now when I realize what he has been and could be - and that I love him. He is the hardest drinker in Goodloets and yet never is drunk. He is soaked from the beginning of one day to another. He began to drink like that the day my mother died and I have always known that *I* was helpless to help him. The weakness was in him, only supported by her strength so long as she was there. He was the most brilliant mind in the state, and was one of the supreme judges when mother died. Now Mr. Cockrell manages his business for him and I have lately come to know that I must sit by and watch him disintegrate. I cannot endure it now, as I have been doing. What is going to help me in this - shame for him? I have gone away to my mother's people to forget and left him to Dabney, and I've come home - to begin the suffering all over. I'll never leave him again. What's going to help me?

And there is something deeper - a race something that fairly eats the heart out of my pride. On almost every page of the history of the Harpeth Valley the name of Powers occurs. One Powers man has been governor of the state, and there have been two United States congressmen and a senator of our house. Father is the last of the line. Because race instinct is the strongest in women, I am the one who suffers as I see my family die out. What is going to help me? A few gospel hymns in a tenor voice the like of which I should have to pay at least three dollars to hear in the Metropolitan? The scene on the porch rose in my mind, but I felt that I both doubted and feared such succor.

And I am in still deeper depths. Nickols is the son of father's first cousin, and has father's full name, Nickols Morris Powers, and he is the last of his branch of the house. Father loves him and is proud of him and nothing ever enters his mind except that I will marry Nickols and start the family all over again. And this is the tragedy. I love Nickols and am entirely unsatisfied with him. He is the Whistler nocturne that my Sorolla nature demands, and he eternally makes me hold out my hand to grasp - nothing. He stands just beyond. I am unable to decide whether he does or does not love me. In New York he lives his life among the artists and fashionable people with whom his highly successful profession throws him, and I don't see why he cares to come back here where he was born and reared, in pursuit of a woman like me. I am as elemental as a shock of wheat back on one of father's meadows and Nickols is completely evolved. He laughs at race pride and resents mine. For six months I had been in New York living with Aunt Clara in Uncle Jonathan Van Eyek's old house down on Gramercy just to go into Nickols' life with him. I went about in the white lights of both Murray Hill and Greenwich Village for about one hundred and eighty-five evenings, and then I fled back to my garden and the poplars - and my anxiety. I thought I had come home to be free and I found the same old chains. And then had come Nickols' telegram of pursuit in the midnight after I had stood by in the shadow and watched a strong man pray and a weak man battle with himself. I was frightened, frightened at the future, and what was going to help me?

"I don't actually understand a word of Gregory Goodloe's sermons, really understand them, I mean, but it helps me to see that somebody truly believes that there is something somewhere that will straighten out tangles - in life as well as thread."

Harriet broke in on my still hunt into my own and other people's inner shrines as she snapped a bit of tangled purple silk thread, knotted it and began all over again on the violet.

"I don't care what he preaches about - he's soothing and I need a little repose in my life after - Oh, what is the matter now?" And as she finished speaking Nell Morgan arose and went with the Suckling asquirm in her arms to meet the large noise that was arriving down the front walk.

The delegation was headed by young Charlotte, whose blue eyes flamed across a very tip-tilted nose that bespoke mischief. Jimmy stolidly brought up the rear with small Sue clinging loyally to his dirty little paddie, which she only let go to run and bury her cornsilk topknot in Harriet's outspread arms, where she was engulfed into safety until only the most delicious dimpled pink knees protruded above dusty white socks and equally dusty white canvas sandals. Though within a few months of four, Sue had discovered Harriet, and never failed to take advantage of her.

"What is the matter?" again demanded Nell, as the vocal chords of Charlotte ceased reverberating and her countenance resumed a more normal color and expression.

"A rock flew and the minister's window got broked." Charlotte gave forth this announcement with a diplomacy that might have been admirable exerted in a juster cause.

"Who had the rock?" demanded the mother sternly.

"Jimmy," was the decided answer, given with a threatening glance at the son of the house of Morgan, who quailed in his socks and sandals and began an attempt to screw one of his toes under one of the flagstones of the walk. I knew in an instant that that rock had never left the hand of small James, but the clash of Nell's wits with young Charlotte is so constant that at times the maternal ones are dulled. The accused must have psychically scented my sympathy, for he lifted large, scared, pleading eyes to mine for a brief second and then dropped them again. I went to the rescue.

"Sue, who broke the window?" I asked, as I extricated the four-year-old witness from Harriet's chiffon and violets. I doubted if young Susan had attained the years of prevarication as yet. I was right.

"Tarlie," was the positive answer. "Boom - book - crk!" was the graphic description of the crash she added as she squirmed back among the violets and the needles and the thread.

"Charlotte!" exclaimed Nell, in real despair.

"Jimmy did have the rock in his pocket, and he just lent it to me to throw at a bird right above the window. It was a nice round one, and he brought it from home to see if he could kill anything. It most killed the minister, and the rock is a little bluggy. Isn't it, Jimmy? He's got it in his pocket for keeps."

"Yes," answered young James, with the brevity with which he usually made responses to the loquacity of his sister.

"Do you mean that you hit Mr. Goodloe, as well as broke the window?" demanded Nell in still more horror, as she came down two of the front steps.

"He didn't mind," answered Charlotte. "He liked it, because he made us both learn a verse of a hymn to sing for punish, and Sue can sing it, too. Come on, Sue!" and before any of us could recover from our horror at the violence the young parson had suffered at the hands of the marauders, Charlotte had lined the other two up on either hand and begun her exhibition of the benefit arising from the throwing of the rock. It was a very good example of the good that may result from evil, which is one of the puzzling reverses of one of the Christian tenets.

"'Work, for the night is coming,
Work through the morning hours,
Work while the dew is sparkling,
Work 'mid springing flowers,'"

trilled Charlotte in a high, buzzy young voice, while Jimmy piped in a few notes lower. Baby Sue's little, clear jumble of words in perfect tune was so bewitchingly sweet that Harriet again engulfed her, while the outraged mother, not so easily beguiled, sailed down the steps and around through the garden toward the chapel, driving the two older offenders before her to the scene of the crime.

"Who is going to help Nell train up liars and murderers into good citizens?" I asked myself in my depths, as I joined with the others in the admiring laugh at young Charlotte's dramatic powers.

"Mr. Goodloe is the most wonderful thing I ever saw with kiddies," said Jessie Litton, as she rose to her feet to begin leave-taking. "Yes, I must go, for father expects me to luncheon," she added, at my remonstrance.

"I'm going to kidnap Sue while I can, and I may never bring her back. I must fly!" said Harriet, and she departed hastily to the small roadster she had parked beside the gate. "Come on, Letitia, and let me take you home," she called over her shoulder, and Letitia followed to secure the short spin around the corner to the old Cockrell home, which was set back from the street behind a tall hedge of waxy-leaved Cherokee roses. Thus almost in the twinkling of an eye I was left alone, which state, however, did not last more than a few seconds, for around the corner of the house from the chapel, from which direction the whole world seemed to be going or coming, arrived Mrs. Elsie Spurlock, beaming the welcome to me that had always found a ready response.

CHAPTER VI

DEEP DIGGING

And in another twinkling of eyes, both of mine and hers, I had taken her bundle from her, seated her in the largest rocking chair, and she had untied her bonnet strings, which denoted that she had come for a genuine visit.

"Well, dearie, dearie me, the sight of you is good for tired eyes, Charlotte," she bumbled in her rich, deep old voice. As she spoke she tucked a white wisp of a curl back into place beneath the second water wave that protruded from under the little white widow's ruche in her bonnet and continued to beam at me. "I met Nellie Morgan and her Annarugans hurrying to pray a pardon from Mr. Goodloe for that rock which might have killed him, if thrown an inch to the right, instead of only nicking that yellow head of his, the Lord be praised!"

"What was that same Lord doing when he let the rock fly from Charlotte's hand to within an inch of the Reverend Mr. Goodloe's life, Mother Spurlock?" I asked her, with the old warfare over the same old subject rising at the very first minute of our meeting. I have wondered sometimes in the last few years if the wrestling with me over her faith was not ordained for the purpose of strengthening Mother Spurlock's powers of patient argument. She is the only person in the world to whom I speak from the depths, and the relief of her sweetened and seasoned wisdom is the straw at which I often clutch to save myself.

"I surmise that He guided the hand of that child so that the verse of the hymn, and the chastisement of the rod I hope Nellie will inflict, might work together for her good. All of us must at times let a little blood for another's good - heart's blood, very often, not just that from our scalps or shins." And as she answered me without a moment's hesitation she enveloped me in loving question. "Are you always going to occupy the anxious seat in front of the Lord, child? Still, sit as long as you like and go on questioning Him. You'll find the answer."

"The whole town seems to have gone into your fold and left me on the 'anxious seat' alone," I answered, as I drew my chair nearer to her and took her lined, strong old hand in mine.

"That Billy Harvey passes the collection plate up the aisle on Sunday and plays poker all Saturday night till Sunday morning down at the Last Chance, in a room in front of the one in which poor Pat Burns, who carries a hod for his money, loses his all. Mary Burns sews all day and half the night to feed him and the children, but she puts her pittance into Billy's plate every Sunday, and I know that she gets the strength to go on from day to day from the words that come from the same pulpit he sets the plate behind. That is, we call the table out at your Country Club a pulpit, until we get our own in the chapel from which to praise the Lord. So you see that there are some sheep who have a taint of goat hair in their wool still left - I won't say with you - out in the world. And speaking of that world, have you come back to say good-bye to us?"

"I don't know yet, Mother Spurlock," I answered her candidly. "I ran away from that world, but it is coming after me on Friday."

"You'll be sent into the vineyard where you are most needed, and there you'll serve," she said, with a far-away look coming into her eyes as she let her glances roam out to the dim hills of Paradise Ridge. A flood of love and reverence rose in my heart for her as I sat quiet and let her spirit roam. Mother Spurlock had been the gayest young matron in Goodloets, living in the great old Spurlock home with handsome, rollicking young George Spurlock for a husband, and three babies around her knees, and in one short year she had been left with only one large and three tiny graves out in the placid home of the dead, beyond the river bend. The babies had been taken by that relentless child foe, diphtheria, and young George, reckless with grief, had let a half-broken horse break his neck. The young woman, aged by her grief, had sold the great house to the next of kin and moved down into an old brick cottage that sat "beside the road" in a gnarled old apple orchard, and had become the "friend to man." Through the orchard and past the door of the Little House ran the path that led from the Settlement to the Town, and through her heart and hands flowed most of the love and charity that bound the rich and poor, brother to brother. Mother Spurlock was never without a bundle in which she carried labor of the poor sold for the gold of the rich, or gifts from the rich back to the needy. I thought of all the long years of service in the vineyard into which her tragedy had thrown her, and I bent and picked up the bundle at our feet and held it with reverent hands.

"Just a few baby things that Nellie Morgan gave me to fix up a poor little Mother Only in the village," she came back from her reverie to say cheerfully, as she saw me with the bundle in my hand. Mother Spurlock always refers to the children without the sanction of the law for their birth as the Mother Onlies, and somehow, when she speaks it, the name carries a world of tenderness into the heart of the hearer.

"Whose now?" I asked her gently, because in a way Mother Spurlock and I bore one another's burdens of spirit.

"Hattie Garrett's, and it's a week old now. It is one of the saddest things that ever happened in the village, and we none of us understand. You remember, she taught the district school down in the Settlement."

"As none of us understood about Martha Ensley. Is that all a mystery still?" I asked, and I stroked the bundle of tiny garments.

"Yes, and now she's gone nobody knows where, day before yesterday. Jacob, her father, was rough and violent with her, but only from grief, and she forgave all that. I'm troubled sorely, for she is gentle, and not one to fight the world alone. She must have gone to the city, the good Lord help her!"

"He will - He is," I answered quickly, then stopped because I knew I must not tell what I had overheard - should I say in the confessional?

"Praise God! to hear you speak such words. Sometimes a body's faith gets out of her heart past her mind and proclaims itself before the higher criticism gets a chance to throttle it," the invincible old warrior exclaimed with a delighted twinkle in her young blue eyes at having caught me with religious goods on me. "He will, He will take *care* of us all, not that He doesn't expect us to put in about sixteen hours of the day helping Him to do it for ourselves and others. That reminds me that I seem to be growing to this chair. Luella May Spain has got a nice place to work in the telegraph station with Mr. Pate, and if she's to look neat she needs a few white shirt waists. I *could* get them in this bundle. If I get too many things from you and Harriet this morning to carry myself, Hampton will take me down the hill in his car when he goes to lunch, not that I wouldn't be frightened to death to ride with him except on the Lord's mission."

"Do you think that fact would keep Hampton from being run down by Harriet when she cuts corners bias, as she insists on doing?" I asked, as I started in the door to procure the toilet necessaries to Luella May's telegraphic career, whether it devastated my supply of tennis clothes or not. Nothing that any woman or any member of her family in Goodloets wears or eats is secure from Mother Spurlock, and we have all submitted to the fact with the greatest docility.

"I know it does; and three shirt waists will be enough if you add a neat black belt," was the answer that followed me through the hall. "Bless my life, Nickols Powers, I was glad to see you at prayer meeting last week, even if you and William Cockrell were just caught up out at your Club in your chess game," I heard her exclaim, to draw a laughing answer in father's most genial rumble. Then I heard him call loudly for Dabney, and when Sallie descended with my bundle, that contained a complete telegraphic outfit for Luella May which showed a decided leaning to tennis style, she met Dabney on the front threshold with a rough parcel from which I saw a shirt sleeve and a blue serge trouser leg protrude.

"Thank you, Nickols. Since his accident, Bill Hanks has thinned out to just about your size. Now he can go back to his job neatly and respectably clad," Mother Spurlock was saying.

"The citizens of Goodloets had better take the habit of wearing a double suit of clothing for fear of having Elsie Spurlock strip them in public to beyond the law," father grumbled in great pleasure, after he had packed her and her bundles in Hampton's car. Father always calls Mother Spurlock "Elsie," and once or twice I have seen a faint blush creep to her cheeks and a glint flash from her eyes, but he blandly goes on doing it. I wonder -

"Father," I said, as we went slowly up the front walk together, "Nickols will be here on Friday; will you have Dabney get his rooms in the north wing ready for him? He likes that light, and he can use the long greenroom for a studio when he sketches."

"That's good," answered father heartily. He likes Nickols and Nickols manages him beautifully, by giving him all he wants to drink whenever he suggests it, even introducing him to new Manhattan beverages. There is perpetual war between Dabney, who knows father's nervous limit, and Nickols, who doesn't care just as long as things and human beings that surround him are kept pleasant. It is all right for the rest of the world to have delirium tremens, just so they do it out of his sight and hearing.

"I wonder just what Nickols will think of Goodloe," father added, with a slightly strained laugh. "You thought he would be enraged at Goodloe and me for building the chapel and weeding the garden. Perhaps he will be unhappy."

"I don't believe your weeding would make anybody unhappy, father," I answered with a laugh, choosing to ignore the issue of the building of the chapel until Nickols was upon the scene and we could decide just what to do.

"Been over the whole garden twice and eaten several meals in the sweat of my brow - that is, I took a cold shower before coming to the table, my daughter," father said, and he looked ashamed of himself for being proud of his own spurt of normality. I caught my breath, but I was wise enough not to show my astonishment. "Goodloe is the most insinuating person I ever met, and I advise you to be careful. He makes men do just as he wants them to, and I should say that women would eat out of his hand."

"I suppose I ought to eat a bite or two from his fingers to pay for all the work he has got out of you and Dabney. I never saw the garden so beautiful or so early. Look, father, the peonies are budding, two weeks ahead of their usual time!"

"They'd be damned ungrateful not to grow industriously, after the way Dab and I have sprained our old backs spading and feeding them according to spiritual direction that stood over us with a rake," answered father, with proud if profane enthusiasm. There was a faint pink glow in his haggard, thin cheeks, and he took from his pocket a huge knife I had never seen him use before and began carefully to cut away a few dead twigs from a budding rose vine.

"Your mother always put a rose from this vine at my plate for breakfast, and you got yours from that pink bush over there by the sun dial," he said, with a softness in his voice that I had not heard since my tenth summer, in which my mother had died. I tingled all over, but held on to myself.

"You go tell that old black lazybones to come here with his spade this minute. I told him about digging in this mulch yesterday before the dahlias sprouted, and he hasn't done it. I'm not going to do it for him, like I put the fertilizer around the lilacs, just to save him from Goodloe. Tell him to come right here to me, and not to let grass grow in his shoe tracks," and father picked up a hoe from the walk beside the neglected dahlias and began doing the work he had just declared against. I fled around to the kitchen, and something lent wings to my feet.

"Oh, Dab, what does it mean that father is really taking an interest in the garden?" I demanded of the faithful old black friend, whom I found enveloped in a kitchen apron helping his wife bring the dinner to a serving head.

"Praise God, his salvation am commenced, if it don't kill me before he gits it," answered Dab, as he put his hand to his back and groaned.

"They has been jest one-half a demijohn of devil heart whisky ordered up outen that cellar in over a month, and I b'lieve this here no account nigger drunk a pint of that," Mammy added to his answer. "Last month it was two demijohns they had up, and before that it was three or four. That parson done it with readin' and talkin' and hoein'. Glory! I wants to hold my breath and shout at the same time, and I would if I could trust this pullet in the skillet to either you or Dabney whilst I did it. The Lord wouldn't listen to no shoutin' from a cook whose chicken was frying black while she did her praisin'," and as she spoke Mammy began a low humming, swaying from table to stove with a rhythm in the swing of her fat body that had a certain dignified beauty to it. It was crude emotion, and I knew it, but I felt it work in my own body as I let the significance of what she had told me about the lessening amount of whiskey father had been consuming add itself to the scene upon the back porch and sink fully into my consciousness. I don't know what might have happened to my shouting Methodist grandmother's worldly though emotional descendant if father's voice, sharp and clear, with a note of command I had forgotten it possessed, had not interrupted me.

"Charlotte! Dab!" it called; and we both answered with all speed.

"That Parson Goodloe have got the power to draw the teeth of seven devils, and you both consider the words of his mouth or he'll git the teeth outen yourn," Mammy called after us in ambiguous warning.

And upon our arrival on the scene of action being executed upon the dahlias, we found the commander of the devils awaiting us, though in his hands was no forked instrument of dentistry, but in one he held a large slice of rye bread thickly spread with butter, and the other was disarmed by a ripe red apple. As we drew near he finished a direction to father and took a huge bite out of the slab of bread that left a gap as wide as one would expect a Harpeth jaguar to make.

"Harrowing deep makes great growth in all plant life," he was saying past the slice of bread with agricultural prosiness to father, who had completely sweated down the very high and stiff collar which he always wore swathed in a wide tie of black after a Henry Clay cut, in a savage attack with the hoe upon the mulch that was smothering the dahlias in richness.

"Does the same deep digging result hold true in biological and psychic life?" puffed father, and then he leaned on his hoe and looked up at the young man towering over him. In his eyes was the appeal of disappointed age calling to the ideals of flaming strength and youth in the deep-jeweled eyes that answered with a look of passionate tenderness as the parson poised the bread for another bite.

"'Whom the Lord loveth He chasteneth,' Mr. Powers, is the direct data we have on that subject," he said. Then he, for the first time, observed the approach of Dabney and myself, of which his widening smile and the quick lowering of the slab of rye pone gave notice to father, who exploded accordingly.

"You black son-of-a-gun! Why didn't you rake off these dahlias as I told you to yesterday? Now you get his hide, Parson!" was the greeting that Dabney received, while I was ignored by all concerned.

"That hinge in your back rusty again, Dabney?" questioned the parson, with leonine mildness.

"I been upsot by my young mistis coming home," answered Dabney, with a quick glance at me as if to indicate me as a substantial excuse for any crimes. I stood convicted, for I do use Dabney continually in all my hospitalities.

"We understand, Dabney," was the answer he got from the feeding Jaguar, who gave me that glint of a laugh that I had learned to expect and to - dread. I knew what he meant to imply, and I also knew that he knew that I understood that he considered me a disturbing element. Then he again raised the half-demolished hunk of bread to his mouth, stopped and regarded the apple in meditative indecision. From head to heels he was clothed in the most exquisite white flannel and buckskin tennis clothes, but for all their civilized worldliness he resembled nothing so much as a feeding king of the forest in the poise of his wonderful head and equally wonderful body. I glanced quickly at his face with its gentle, deep, comprehending lines, in positive fear of him, and I found reassurance in the smile that curled his strong red mouth and glinted at me from his brilliant eyes under dull gold. Then, after the smile, he decided for the apple rather than further conversation, and was just going to set his white teeth in its rosy cheek when I stopped him with an almost involuntary exclamation.

Maria Thompson Daviess

"Don't!" I pleaded. "Dinner is just ready, and you'll spoil it if you eat all that bread and butter and apple." Just exactly a week before, at almost that exact hour, the Reverend Gregory Goodloe had refused the cup of tea I had stood holding for him in my hand for five minutes on the front porch of the Poplars, and I had taken a resolve that never would he again receive a food invitation from me. I didn't count Mammy's "snack" eaten on the Harpeth adventure. I didn't understand myself and my sudden rush of dismay at the idea of a spoiled dinner for him, but I couldn't stop myself as I added:

"Mammy has apple dumplings and hard sauce; please don't - I mean please *do* come in to dinner with us."

"Thank you, but as you see I've about dined," he answered me, as with a laugh he held out his fragments. "Jefferson was feeling badly and I sent him to bed instead of the parsonage kitchen." Mammy had told me that the Reverend Mr. Goodloe had taken hers and Dabney's cherished and perfectly worthless only son as his sole domestic dependence, and Mammy had added the fact that Jeff had "shot nary crap since the parson rescued him from the jaw of the jail."

"Huh," ejaculated Dabney over the hoe he had taken from father and was using at his direction while father lined the border beside the bed with his sharp spade. I knew the contempt in his voice was for the illness of Jefferson, and the Reverend Mr. Goodloe and I both laughed as he took the last bite of the brown slab and then held out the unbitten side of the apple to me.

"You eat your fruit with me, not in dumplings with hard sauce," he said, and there was a wooing note in his voice as if he pleaded for that friendliness from me to heal a hurt.

"No, *I* won't eat out of your hand," I answered, with a cool emphasis on the "I." And I looked him straight in the eyes, for I wanted him to know that I had thoroughly understood his refusal of my invitation couched so gently, but which I considered in reality haughty and resentful, especially as I had been his guest in his car. "We'll wait until you get your shower, father, and not much longer," I said to father, as I turned and went along the flagstones to the steps that led to the balcony upon which opened the long windows of the dining room. I was furious and I was hurt.

At times I become acutely conscious that I am very imperious, but it is not entirely my fault. My friends have depended upon my clear head, in which father's brain seems to work with a kind of feminine vigor, and I have always felt that the superior force with which I have loved and cherished them made it all right. I've always stood by them and used myself mercilessly for their exigencies, and I suppose I have ruled them as mercilessly. I rarely encounter another will, and to clash into one as strong as mine drew the sparks of my nature. The blaze was soon over, but I - smouldered.

During dinner I was deeply interested in father's plans for my garden, which brilliantly carried the plans Nickols and I had made to what I saw in another year would be a marvelously artistic completeness. But under the joy of hearing him talk as I had never really heard him since I was old enough to appreciate his scintillating delicious choice of words and phrases, I was hot and sore at the thought of my duty to render gratitude where gratitude was due for having him like that.

"It will be perfectly wonderful, father, and Nickols had not worked it out to anything like that completeness. He will be wild about it, but won't it take a lot of money? And where did you get your inspiration?" I asked the question, though I hated the answer I knew it must receive.

"The plans are entirely my own," answered father, with a pleased flush making even brighter his dulled eyes and cheeks, faintly glowing from the shower at which Dabney had officiated a few minutes before. I had not failed to notice that we had sat down and were halfway through dinner and father's hand had not motioned Dabney towards the decanter and ice and siphon on the sideboard. "I must confess that the inspiration came from a kind of rage when Goodloe said to me how much it was to be regretted that all the great gardens in the North are being made out of a sort of patchwork of English, French, Italian and even Japanese influences. You couldn't expect anything more of the inhabitants of the part of the country in the veins of whose people flow just about that mixture of blood, but in the Harpeth Valley we have been Americans for two and a half centuries, and I'll show 'em an American garden if it does unhinge both mine and Dabney's backs and make Cockrell swear I'm crazy when he audits my accounts once every month. No, Madam, your own grandmother and great-grandmother, in conjunction with Goodloe's maternal ancestors, conceived and laid out the beginning of the great American garden, and we will combine to produce it."

"What about Nickols' plans?" I asked, trying hard to raise indignation in my heart and voice at the thought of Nickols Morris Powers' work, for which the people of wealth in the North were beginning fairly to clamor, being criticized and laid aside at the inspiration of the Methodist parson across the lilac hedge. And I succeeded better than I expected, for I saw father lose color and tremble with his own rage, which he always quells with drink.

"That sunken garden is Italian, and I'm going to tear it out and put - Oh, my daughter; forgive me, but I forgot, in this queer nature frenzy that has come over me of late and which I do not at all understand, that the garden is yours, was your mother's and grandmother's. So far the plans have just been begun, and nothing that you and Nickols have done - Dabney, pour me three fingers of the 1875 Bourbon." And in a second I saw father grow white and shaking with mortification at what he felt to be an unmannerly trespass upon another's rights. My father has been a drunkard for nearly twenty years, but he is still a great gentleman. Slowly he drank the whiskey, every drop of which seemed to go to my heart like cold lead.

"But, father!" I exclaimed, determined to win him back. Dabney was putting the silver stopper in the decanter over by the sideboard, and I thought I saw a sob shake his bent old shoulders as his black hands trembled. "I'd like to know if I'm not as purely American as you are, and have I not the same right to want, demand and work for an American nationalism, even in a garden, as you have? I'll have you know, sir, that the future of the nation is in the hands of the women. We can produce pure Americans or let the whole country go hybrid." And as I spoke I let my temper rise to a point which I hoped would shock father and take his mind from the decanter and the ice. "I demand that you allow me to carry out your plans for my garden, and that you help me do it to the limit of the hinges in your back and Dabney's. And, Dabney, don't let me hear another word about that hinge until those dahlias are in bloom. Also get me a half dozen bottles of dynamite to blow out that Italian garden. I never did like it."

"Yes'm," answered Dabney, meekly but comprehendingly, for he hastily flung a napkin over the ice and gently set the decanter back in its rack. "But dynamite, it comes in sticks and not in bottles. And it would shake the roots of them old poplars clean most down to hell."

"How'll we get that sunken garden out, then, father?" I asked, and I saw the life and color come back to his face in a flood of humor.

"We might try filling it in," he answered, and then we both laughed at ourselves, with Dabney joining in.

CHAPTER VII

THE TRISTAN LOVE SONG

After dinner father and I sat out on the porch in the soft, warm breeze that waved a misty spring moonlight around us, and talked garden until after ten o'clock. He was brilliant and delightful, but three times he made trips to ice bowl and decanter on the sideboard.

"It will be a great relief and happiness to me if Nickols does sanction and set the seal of artistic approval upon our plans," he said, with feverish but happy eyes. "You see, Nickols will represent the cosmopolitan in judgment upon the normally developed insular. I remember once that Mr. Justice Harlan said that in an opinion on freight rates I had sent up to him I had represented both the cosmopolitan and the insular interest with astonishing equity, and I told him that I considered that it took at least six generations of insular mind culture to see any kind of national equity. The same thing holds good with a garden. It takes the sixth generation on a piece of land to produce a garden, and then it has to be laid out around a library full of the ideals of poet and scholar. In about three years I can, with your permission, present the American nation with a garden that will represent the best ideals of Americans; and I must go to bed if I expect to get up and hunt the early worm. I can never decide which is the harder work, the capture of that creature of tradition or the arousing of Dabney to perform that task. You, Dabney."

"Yes, sir," came a sleepy groan from just within the door, and in a second the old black face was lit up with father's candle until the white wool above shone like a halo as it appeared from out the gloom. And I sat and watched the two old gentlemen, one black and one white, toil slowly up the steps and down the wide hall of the Poplars.

"Father *must* come back; the nation needs him," I said fiercely under my breath as I noticed that in Dabney's hand swung the ice bucket where I had been accustomed to see it swing for years, but which I had not seen him carry before since I came home. "And that's how *you* help him fight to come back," I arraigned myself with bitter scorn. "You have no faith nor spiritual sources yourself, and you throw him back into degradation when something is helping him crawl out. What's helping him? No matter what it is, you are a coward to obstruct it."

And for a long hour I sat thus raging at myself and questioning hopelessly, while the young moon rose higher and higher over the tops of the silvery poplars and young spring slipped about in the lights and shadows, invisible except for perfumed wreathings of gossamer mist. Above, I heard father pacing up and down his rooms, slowly, almost feebly. Sometimes he would hesitate; then I would hear him stop beside the window, where I knew the ice bowl and the decanter were placed upon a table which had stood beside the head of his bed so burdened since my early childhood. I had always dreaded his moroseness and instinctively felt the cause of it. I had never really loved him until just the last few days, and now I felt my love rise in a tide that threatened to overwhelm me.

"Oh, I found him, and now I've thrown him away," I sobbed to myself. Then, as I sat listening, I heard the faltering steps come out into the hall above, descend the steps one by one, go through the dark dining room groping pitifully, and down the side steps out into the beloved garden. Silently I watched the tall figure with the white hair silvered radiantly by the moonlight go slowly down the path, past the old graybeard poplars, and even up to the lilac hedge that ran as a bulwark in front of the dark chapel door, which I could see was ajar as it always is.

"He's going for help," I muttered to myself, and I felt the padding of fear pursuing me, while also something of the Methodist grandmother within me began a queer calling and a tightening at my throat.

Then something happened that interested me so that I lost all personal anxiety. Father stopped beside the hedge and picked up something from the grass. I saw it was a long, heavy hoe. Walking over to a long bed of early roses he and Dabney had been fertilizing in the late afternoon, he bent feebly and began to dig the food into their roots. As he swung the long handle, each blow upon the soft earth became more decided. I crept down behind the old snowball bush to be nearer him; I didn't dare go to him in his fight, because I had in my selfish heed-lessness brought it all on, but in a little while he was not alone, for a bent old figure with grizzled white wool sticking out from under a red flannel nightcap came quietly along the path with a hoe in his hand, fell in directly behind his master, and began a rhythmic blow-answering-blow contest with the fragrant earth and the demon within the man. For at least an hour the two old friends worked up and down the long bed, until I could see father begin to totter with weakness.

"Now, come on, Mas' Nick, honey, and go to bed. I'll pour a bucket of cistern water over you and rub you down so as you'll sleep like a bug in a rug," the staunch old comrade crooned, with a mother note in his voice, as he took father's heavy hoe and shouldered it with his.

"I think evening exercise is good for me, Dabney," answered father with all the dignity and command come back into his voice. "Put both those hoes in the tool house this time, and I'll not tell Mr. Goodloe you left one down by the lilac hedge."

"Yes, sir, thanky, sir, fer not telling him," answered Dabney, as he followed his master to the tool house under the back steps, deposited the garden implements where he was directed, and then again followed his idol in through the long dining room window and was lost in the shadow.

I went back to the front steps, again sank down, put my arms on my knees, and let my head fall upon my clasped hands. As I sat there alone, with the dark house yawning behind me in its emptiness, someone sat down beside me and laid a warm, strong hand on my interlaced and strained fingers for just about half a second.

"Please forgive me about the apple dumplings and the hard sauce," a merry, very lovely voice pleaded.

"I went out to Old Harpeth with you when you asked me; but I loathe going to church - I haven't been in one since I was strong enough to rebel - and I'm not going to yours," was the apology I graciously offered in return for that about the apple dumplings. "But I'd pay fifty dollars for a tenth row seat to hear you sing Tristan in the Metropolitan any day if I had to go hungry for a week to pay for it," I added, as I laughed as softly as he had pleaded. All the sorrow and strain of the last hours had vanished at the touch of his hand, and I felt like an impish, teasing child.

"I'll sing some of it for you now, if you'll give fifty cents to Mother Spurlock for the Children's Day Picnic. And it'll be a bargain you are getting," was the unexpected offer I encountered.

"And a freezer of vanilla ice cream to boot," I assented, generously.

And then something happened to me the like of which I know never happened to anybody in all the world, and that could happen only the once to me. Gregory Goodloe drew a little closer to me and bent his great gold head until his face was just off my left shoulder, and in his powerful, rich, fascinating voice, which he muted down in a way that made it sound as if he were singing through a golden cloud, he sang Tristan's immortal love agony in a way that shut out all the rest of the universe and left me alone with him in a space swayed by his pleading until my mortal body shook in actual pain.

"Don't! I can't stand it!" I gasped, as I seized his wrist in my strong hands and wrung it. "Stop!"

The last tender note breathed itself into the air that seemed to hold it in a long caress until it died away, and sobs shook me as I held on desperately to his wrist. I felt that I *must* be comforted. And I was! Again the gentle fingers were laid over mine for a still smaller fraction of a second, and then again the beautiful, clear voice began to sing to me, just to me, out of the whole world.

"'Abide with me, fast falls the even tide,'" he chanted, and then waited while my sobs died away and I let go my drowning grasp on his wrist.

"That's just what I mean. That's just why I wouldn't have any more respect for myself if I should go to your church than if I joined in one of Mammy's foot-washings down at the river and fell in a fit of shouting in which it took two burly coons to 'hold my spirit down,' as she describes those gymnastics to me. I hate you and I hate my friends for indulging in religion, because it is just as 'potent an agent of intoxication' as exists to-day, and it blinds us to the need of work along scientific lines for the immediate improvement of the race. What right have we to intoxicate reason with religion? If religion is anything it must be reason." I fairly hurled my words of half-baked skepticism at him, with the vision of father and Dabney digging in the garden, still in my eyes.

"I felt just as you do about it a year ago to-day," he answered me quietly. "As you state the case of religion as emotion versus reason, it doesn't exist. Religion is reason plus emotion, and when you combine the two the eyes of your soul are open, whereas they had been closed. Nobody can tell you about it, but you begin really to live when you see and comprehend. Yes, it is going to take all the scientific reason the world possesses to start its salvation, but it will not get far without 'emotion,' as you call what I *know* is love of God, and, through that love, compassion for man."

"The assumption that every man is blind who does not believe as you do, stops all argument," I said scornfully.

"I didn't come to talk religion with you; I came over to get that apple dumpling off my conscience, as I couldn't digest it because it wasn't there. I preach twice, on Sunday and on Wednesday night, and I'm in my study behind the altar every afternoon that I'm not playing tennis. I'll be there any time by appointment." The worldly and protective raillery in that young Methodist minister's voice almost interrupted my religious researches, but I was in depths that were strange to me, and I was floundering for a line out.

"I'll never be there," I flared at him, then went on with my floundering. "If a man is blind, how can he gain the sight that you arrogate to yourself?"

"A great man once prayed, 'Lord, help thou my unbelief,'" was the gentle answer in which was that queer note of apostolic surety with which I heard him address the woman in the garden that night.

"I can't pray - there's nothing there," I said in a very small voice that I could scarcely recognize as my own. "Oh, I mean that we are all floundering, and where can we get the lifeline? Where did you get the line that you think will pull you out of the vortex?"

Then for a long moment he and I sat again involved in the emptiness of the universe that Tristan's love song had opened for us, and I knew that with ruthless feet I had entered his Holy of Holies and was being allowed to stand across the threshold.

"Forgive me," I gasped.

"I never felt that I could tell it before," he said, slowly, and the bounds of the emptiness retreated still further away as he turned so that he sat facing me and again bent his dull gold head closer to mine. In a second I knew why in my mind I had been calling him a Harpeth jaguar. It was just my pictorial expression for the word freedom, the freedom that comes from power. I knew that mentally and bodily I was looking upon the first free man I had ever encountered, and I was abashed.

"Don't tell me," I said, with a gentleness in my voice I had never heard before, and that came from something that I felt to be strangely like meekness, though I had never before met that emotion in myself.

"You know the romance of my father's life," the soft voice went on, speaking as if I had not interrupted him, "but nobody knows the tragedy. Love for my mother came upon him like an arrow shot out of ambush, and he married into a worldly, pleasure-loving, agnostic circle of people who all adored and flattered him until he - he became confused and doubting. He had transgressed the law: 'yoke not yourselves with unbelievers,' and he suffered. She never understood. It killed him, and when he had been dead nearly twenty years I found the diary he kept the months before he died. It was last year, just after her death. It was a cry to me, who at that time was a mere babe, and it - it lighted the flame he had almost let go out. As I read, the apostolic call came to me and I answered. I was starting to the front in France, and I went on. My year there was a series of experiences that gave me my surety. One day it came more clearly than ever. I had gone out into one of the trenches of the first line, because I am so strong that I can carry any man back to the stretchers across my back or in my arms. I have carried two at a time. There were nineteen men in the trench, and I made the twentieth. Suddenly a machine gun found the range and mowed them all down like cornstalks or wheat heads. Only I was left standing, bleeding under my left ribs. I raised my voice and praised God for my surety of immortality, and then fell. While I was practically dying in the hospital with a clip in my lung I got suddenly and unaccountably well and strong, and felt I must come back to try and help others to see what we must see to assure every man of his immortality. When the race awakens to that fact there will be no more use for machine guns. I may not help much, but I can only try. Perhaps I do only work through the emotions as yet, but I believe that my ministry will have its fruits. I can wait." And the humility and patience in his voice beat against my heart and bruised it so that I cried out.

"Oh, why did you come here?" I positively moaned, as he and I both rose and I put out my hand as if to force him out of that aloneness in which we stood together.

"America must lead the world in spiritual as well as material regeneration, and this is the only real and dispassionate America, with no foreign pull on its vitals. You must wake up; the cry has been heard to 'Come over and help.' Why do you fight the -"

"I can't help fighting. I must do what I conscientiously believe -" I was saying with my hand still outstretched against him, when suddenly the still place around us was invaded with a crash and its invisible walls thrown down.

"Charlotte!" came in Nickols' languid, fascinating voice that always draws me to the edge of his world. "And Greg Goodloe, by all that is good and holy - in tennis flannels!"

CHAPTER VIII

BREASTING THE GALE

In the radiant moonlight I saw the lithe muscles of the Jaguar grow taut and stiff, and I felt rather than saw his long, strong hands clench themselves. I was about to stretch out my arms and ward off something that seemed like danger to Nickols, standing down at the bottom of the steps, smiling up at us in the moonlight with his mocking, fascinating smile, when suddenly the anger seemed to flow away from the body of the parson and he smiled down into the upturned eyes with great gentleness as we started down the steps together.

"I didn't interrupt the salvation of Charlotte's soul, did I?" Nickols asked, as he took my outstretched hand in his left hand and raised it to his lips as he held out his right to the Reverend Mr. Goodloe. So real had been that fraction of an instant when I had stood between the two men that I almost felt the sensation of alarm a second time as I saw Nickols' slender, magical, artist's fingers laid in the slim, powerful hand of the Reverend Mr. Goodloe, but the gentle voice reassured me as the Harpeth Jaguar answered the intruder, or what he must have felt to be the intruder, for I had something of that feeling myself at the advent of my lover at the moment he had chosen for his arrival.

"The trouble began about apple dumplings and hard sauce," I said, as quickly as my wits would act.

"How are you, Nickols Powers, since we separated 'somewhere in France,' you with your sketch books and I with my hospital stretchers? I got a dandy lung clip; did you bring away any lead?" And the parson's voice was gentle and cordial and full of a laughing reminiscence.

"Didn't smell powder after I left you," answered Nickols, as we all ascended the steps and stood in a group before the door. "I got my books full of sketches of bits of treasures that the war might destroy, and beat it back to civilization. Did the Madonna of the Red Cross you had in tow come across as sentimentally as was threatened?" Nickols' voice was as cordial as the Reverend Goodloe's, but something in me made me resent the question and the manner it was asked.

"She was killed in a field hospital just a few weeks after we left her - 'somewhere in France.' She got God's welcome!" was the answer that came to the laughing question in a quiet, reverent voice. And as he spoke the parson started down the steps, then turned for his farewell.

"That - or sweet oblivion," said Nickols, as he came to the edge of the steps and looked down at the Harpeth Jaguar coolly. I again got the sense of danger from the tall, lithe figure that stood in the moonlight, radiant before us in the shadow. "We'll contest that point warmly while we contest the meeting house Charlotte writes me that you planted in our garden - of Eden."

"I can contest - if I must," was the serene answer that came back at us from over the white silk-clad shoulder. "Good night, both of you, and I hope to see you both again soon. Smell the lilacs bursting bud in your garden - of Eden!" With which farewell he left us to our greetings.

"That's some man to be lost in the ranks of the shibboleths," said Nickols with generous ease, as we watched the last glint of the moon on the yellow head disappearing around the corner. "Degrees from three old colleges, millions, women lovers in

Maria Thompson Daviess

millions, all thrown away to sing psalms for a few rustics in little old Goodloets. Can you beat it? But, blast him, he can't take away my loving welcome with his fatal beauty," and as he spoke, with a tender laugh Nickols held out his arms to me. I went into them and he held me close.

"I couldn't stay away - with Goodloe and the meeting house in the ring against me," he whispered, and he tried to raise my head for the kiss I had been holding from him all the long winter of our engagement, claiming to want it only under the roof of the Poplars. I burrowed my face in his shoulder and held to him with such fervor that it was impossible for him to raise my head.

"Not yet," was my muffled pleading.

"Again, damn that huge blond giant for being in the way of my getting my own on the first-sight wave," said Nickols with a good-humored laugh, as he pushed me from him. "Take your time. I like ripe fruit - and kisses. Did you say Goodloe had come over to steal apple dumplings and you had caught him in the act? I never was so hungry before and one of Mrs. Dabney's apple dumplings with that hard sugar stuff smothered with cream - well, of course I could wait until breakfast, but I'd be mighty weak. Your night train carries no dining car."

"I feel sure that there is at least a half panful in the pantry; let's go see," I answered with delight at the practical turn the scene had taken, and I led him into the dark house, turned on one or two lights and went with him back into the culinary department of the Poplars.

And as I had predicted so we found the larder supplied. With a huge plate of the pastry encrusted apples, smothered with all the cream from one of Mammy's pans of milk, and a tall bottle from the sideboard, Nickols led the way out of the long windows onto the south balcony over which the moon, now high in the heavens, poured the radiance of a new-toned daylight. I followed him with some glasses and sugar and a bowl of cracked ice that I had found in its usual place in the corner of the refrigerator.

"Pretty good substitute for the affectionate sweet I thought of all the way down from New York," said Nickols with an adorable laugh, as he lifted the first spoonful, dripping with cream, to his mouth. Then with the food almost bestowed he paused and looked out beyond the garden toward the chapel, which loomed up gray and shimmering in the silver light.

"Great heavens!" he ejaculated, and for a long minute the spoon was poised while his eyes fairly devoured the scene spread out before him against the background of Paradise Ridge.

"If you don't like it we can get rid of it," I said, as I poured his drink over the ice tinkling against the side of the glass.

"Not like it!" exclaimed Nickols, as he rose with the spoonful of dumplings dashed back into the plate. "That is the most wonderful and beautiful landscape effect I have ever beheld. That is just what our garden needed. I suppose I would have seen it and put some sort of a pavilion there, but that squat and perfect old church would have been beyond me."

"Oh, I'm glad!" I exclaimed, as he sank back on the step beside me, took the glass from my hand, drank deeply and this time began a determined attack upon the plate in his hand. And then as he ate I told him all about father and his plans for the garden and his own improvement and to what I hoped the work was leading him. But somehow I couldn't bring myself to describe the scene which had that night been enacted in the garden - I couldn't. "Oh, I am so glad you are not furious and will maybe be willing to encourage him, even if it does mean to encourage the Methodist Church and the minister thereof. You are wonderful, Nickols," I finished with a squeeze of his arm that very nearly jostled the cream out of the spoon upon his gray tweed trousers.

"I'd be a wonderful ass not to take advantage of Judge Nickols Powers' brain and money, plus Gregory Goodloe's brain and training and money combined, to get a result that will be worth a hundred thousand dollars to me and all the fame I can conveniently wear. Encourage 'em? Just watch me! Only what the judge thinks will take two years can be done in one season if we get experts down to do it, which we will. Trees two hundred years old *can* be moved for a few thousand dollars, as well as plants in bloom that would require years to transplant. I know the man to do it: Wilkerson of White Plains. I'll telegraph him in the morning."

"He won't interfere with - with father, will he?" I asked anxiously.

"Not a bit - he'll just make what the judge and Gregory plan for year after next, grow and bloom there in a couple of months. Wilkerson is not a creator, he's just nature keyed up to the *n*th power. And also I'll give him for a bait the Jeffries estate I was hesitating about making a bid for. All the big fellows are after it. Old man Jeffries has made two barrels of money in the last ten years in oil and he is going to build an estate up on the Hudson that will make the world gasp. I hadn't put in a bid, but this idea of the judge's and Greg's, with the whole village grouped about it, has given me the keynote to win the thing from the whole bunch of American architects. He wants the village built as well as the estate. That American garden idea will bowl him over. He's progressively and rabidly American. The bids don't close until December, so I'll have time to get real photographs and sketches. Me for the reformed judge and the parson!"

"This is the most wonderful thing I ever heard and I want father pushed to the limit with the planning. I don't care where the parson comes in, just so I don't have to join the church to get the garden," I said, as I tinkled the ice in Nickols' empty glass, while he consumed the last bit of cream from the empty plate.

"Oh, I'll join the church if it is needed to push the garden," said Nickols with a laugh, as he lit a cigarette and puffed a smoke ring out toward the gray little chapel. "Most people who join churches do it for some kind of pull, social or business, or a respectability stamp or to be white-washed. I'll put on a frock coat and pass the plate if it will help the parson evolve another phase of gardenism."

"Billy gets home from his poker game at the Last Chance, down in the Settlement, on Sunday morning, just in time to bathe and get into his frock coat to perform that office," I said with a laugh that had a hint of recklessness tinged with contempt.

"I'll see Billy through both ceremonials," said Nickols. "Has Billy come into the fold?"

"He has! So have all the rest," I answered. "I am the only black sheep and they are all backsliding down on me. I am getting, and will get, the blame of it all as a corrupter of public morals."

"Why don't you join and then do as you please with the official stamp of Christianity upon you?" Nickols asked, as he puffed comfortably away in the moonlight.

One of the things that cause me the deepest hurt is to try to get Nickols to look down into my depths and read one, just any one, of the hieroglyphics there. I know each time I open my nature to him he is going to turn aside, and yet I will try. As his arm stole around me I made another one of the attempts that I always know beforehand are doomed to failure.

"There is something in me, a quality of mind that seems to be judicial, which insists that as a cold scheme for existence in this universe nothing compares with that of life followed by eternal redemption through personal effort interpreted by a mediator. The bare Christian tenets have a nobility that it kills me to see belittled by the bored, half-hearted observances of most of its

Maria Thompson Daviess

protestants, who in turn are not to be blamed for being half-hearted and bored by the dogmas and restrictions and littleness with which the great bare scheme has been enmeshed and clothed. The Methodist Church positively forbids Billy to play poker or drink, but it just as positively forbids him to see Pavlowa dance or Beerbohm Tree play Falstaff or Forbes Robertson incarnate Hamlet. And look at its wretched machinery - they allow a young man to give his life and expect inspiration from him at six hundred dollars a year with a wife and two dozen children, which he has been encouraged to bring down upon himself, dependent on that same six hundred dollars. The great men who are expected to direct our spiritual destinies don't get as much money as many ordinary grocers and certainly not enough to support their obligations with dignity. What is true of the Methodist Church is true of all the rest, in perhaps a greater degree. So with their smallness and their pettiness and their befogging stupidity I feel that they may be denying thinkers like you and me the use of their scheme and we'll have to find another for ourselves if we want immortality."

"Do we want that immortality?" asked Nickols easily. "This world is a pretty good old place if you don't regard the 'shalt nots,' but isn't it long enough to live the allotted time? What do we want to do it all over again for, that is, provided we do all the pleasant things while we have the chance? I don't want to see any play twice, even a masterpiece. I wouldn't want to live again unless I had been a Christian in this life and felt that I wanted to come back and do a lot of the things I had just heard about and previously hadn't tried."

"Certainly I wouldn't want another life that is as unsatisfied as this," I murmured, more to myself than to Nickols.

"Do the things that satisfy," he urged again, and I could see a deviltry dancing at me out of the corner of his eyes that I resented deeply without exactly knowing why.

"Harriet Henderson can't get Mark Morgan's love or - his

children, and Nell Morgan is unattainable for Billy. Though they have all the world's goods and go a pace that pleases them, they are unsatisfied. If they don't get the new deal that immortality promises they lose the whole thing," I answered straight out from the shoulder. "And what about those who die in infancy and - and you and me?"

"If you'll just kiss me and hush preaching to me I'll be entirely satisfied and ready to die as soon as I have lifted that fifty thousand out of old Jeffries with the judge's and the Reverend Gregory's garden and done a few more commissions. Try kissing me and see if you don't feel more cheerful," Nickols answered with a laugh, as he drew me close to him. I sadly shut up the doors of my depths, warded off the kiss - why, I didn't know - and persuaded him to go up to his rooms which I had seen Sallie and Dabney put in order that afternoon.

It was midnight when I parted with Nickols at the head of the old winding stairs in the fragrant darkness, lit only by the silver light of the night from a long window at the front of the hall. He held me close for a half second as he whispered:

"Let me make you happy. I understand."

"I don't understand, and until I do I'd make you miserable, dear," I whispered back as I drew myself out of his reluctant arms and went into my own door.

Then for a long midnight hour I stood at my deep window and looked out over the garden, past the squat steeple silvering beyond the lilac hedge, to Paradise Ridge in the dim distance, and tried to read my own hieroglyphics. I needed help. Nickols had come after me to Goodloets in a spirit of gentle determination and I knew the fight would be to the finish. And why should I fight? Any woman ought to be proud to marry Nickols Morris Powers, especially a woman who had loved him since her heart had been developed to the knowledge of love. Very unostentatiously and with perfect good taste Nickols had let me see that Marie VanClive with her

Knickerbocker ancestry and her Manhattan land-grants fortune was very decidedly interested in him in her cultured and perfected young way, and young Mrs. Houston had herself shown me the same thing on one of the week-end flights we had had on her yacht. And beyond all that my own heart told me that Nickols was desirable. His gentleness and his tenderness and his daring and his humor were irresistible to a woman. And his lazy acquiescence in life was peaceful and inviting to my own strenuosity. I felt as if I had always been an eagle breasting the gale with no place to alight, and now Nickols was calling to me from an eyrie on a mountain side to come and rest and be mated and comforted.

"I'm tired of loneliness and I think I'll drift and be happy," I murmured, as I fell asleep with my back to the silver steeple against the dim hills.

CHAPTER IX

INTO BRAMBLES

The next morning I awoke with the same resolve in my heart, to be happy if wicked, and proceeded to execute it with a great vigor. And in the execution of that resolve dear old Goodloets almost had some of the moss of its century's repose scraped off of its back.

First and foremost, we all danced, day and night. We had really begun the giddy whirl the summer before when we had built the little clubhouse over in the oak grove by the river's edge, just between the Town and the Settlement, so that we would no longer feel the limit and limitations to our gliding of anybody's double parlors, and conservative Goodloets had been duly shocked thereat.

"Ladies did not dance outside of their own and their friends' private homes in my day," Mrs. Cockrell had sighed, as she finished the petal of the rose she was embroidering upon some of Letitia's lingerie.

"I'd rather they danced in their den of iniquity than to execute these modern gyrations in my home," had responded Harriet's mother, Mrs. Sproul, as she finished the hundredth round on the shawl she was knitting. Harriet's report of the conversation had been received with great hilarity that evening at dinner at the Club.

Maria Thompson Daviess

But Goodloets had had a year in which to recover from the shock of the institution of the Country Club when I started in to enjoy myself. Having church services there on Sundays and Wednesdays during the winter had done much to remove the prejudice in the minds of the conservative. I suspected the Reverend Mr. Goodloe of a great deal of worldly wisdom when I saw how he had been able to persuade the directors, Hampton Dibrell and Mark and Cliff, to let him do such a weird thing. Mrs. Sproul and Mrs. Cockrell and their friends had first been tolled out to prayer meeting and then had come to witness a tennis match. Billy, in great glee, recounted to me the first time they had stayed to dinner with him and father and Mr. Cockrell. They had been enjoying the prayer meetings to the utmost and had come out with Mother Spurlock by mistake on a Tuesday night, which was the regular dinner dance night. It was some time before they discovered their mistake, for they were immensely enjoying their visit with Mother Spurlock, and when the dancing began Billy had seized Mother Elsie in his arms and danced her the whole length of the room. The music had been too much for her feet in their sensible shoes, and very suddenly they had unfolded their wings after thirty long years of rest and had fairly flown up and down and backwards and forwards with Billy's in a sedate version of one of the phases of the tango. Mrs. George Spurlock had been the best dancer in Goodloets when time was young.

"Do you think that it was the devil that tempted you, Mother Elsie?" I asked her about it one day when she had a leisure moment for teasing.

"Effie Burns' youngest baby was born exactly while I was dancing, and we will have six months' trouble with her because her band was not put on properly," was her answer, as she took up her parcel of five pairs of only slightly worn stockings that five girls in the Settlement needed worse than I needed darns, and departed in a great hurry. "Oh, but you should have seen Hattie Sproul's eyes while I danced," she called back over her shoulder as she went through the gate.

And so in the second summer of the Club's existence there had been no bridle upon its gayeties - I had almost used the word license, and I suppose it would have been a just one under the circumstances. Billy called it "The Bucket of the Lost Lid," and every individual member did exactly as he or she chose. The sideboard out on the back porch made as good a bar as any in the state with old Uncle Wilks to officiate, and in the wing in one of the private dining rooms a huge wheel stood with its face to the wall during the day, but came complacently out of its corner when night descended. On the porch could always be found either Mrs. James Knight or Mrs. Buford Cunningham. They neither of them had children, hated home and were serenely happy sitting on the front porch knitting silk scarfs and gossiping with all comers, while James and Buford hung around the sideboard at the back. They were institutions and all of the unmarried boys and girls, men and women, widowed and widowered, came and went at will, with the liberty that the chaperonage of their certain presence allowed.

"Suppose one of 'em should fall dead and the other have to attend her funeral," Nickols remarked one Saturday night at a dinner table not more than twelve feet away from the two couples. "The scandal that would soon disrupt this town for lack of their free chaperonage would be like an earthquake. None of you would have a shred of respectability with which to drape yourselves to appear in public."

"They don't wear much respectability anyway in the eyes of the Settlement," said Billy, as he mixed the champagne cup with old Wilks standing admiringly by. "The floor manager ordered Luella May Spain off the floor at the dance they had in the lodge room over the Last Chance last Saturday night for appearing in one of Harriet's last year dancing frocks Mother Spurlock had collected for her, though they do say that Luella May had sewed in two inches of tucker and put in sleeves. How's that for an opinion passed upon the high and mighty from the meek and lowly?"

"I'd been in mourning a year. That was my coming out gown

and I felt -" Harriet was saying when Billy laughed and interrupted her.

"And you came out, Harriet dear," he assured her, as he poured her champagne cup and his and signaled Wilks to serve the rest of us.

On the surface all of the joy that most of Goodloets was having was real and brilliant and spontaneous, all the dancing and drinking and high playing, but under the surface there were dark currents that ran in many directions. Young Ted Montgomery and Billy played poker one Saturday night until daylight out at the Club, and Bessie Thornton and Grace Payne had "staid by" and were having bacon and eggs with them when the sun rose. Judge Payne, Grace's father, has been a widower ten years and Grace, with the four younger "pains," as Billy calls them, has run wild away from him and her grandmother, old Madam Payne, who lives in a world of crochet needles and silk thread with Mrs. Cockrell and Mrs. Sproul. One night I went with Billy in his car to take Grace home and he had to wait until I tiptoed to her room with my arm around her and put her to bed, while Harriet was doing the same thing with Bessie Thornton. Those girls are not much over twenty and they are only a little more "liberated," as they call it, than the rest of their friends. Ted Montgomery loves Grace, when he is himself and not at the card table, but what chance have they to form a union of any solidity and permanence? Billy's nephew, Clive Harvey, has always loved Bessie Thornton, but he is teller in the Goodloets bank and almost never sees her. He is one of the stewards in the Harpeth Jaguar's church, and the suffering on his slim young face hurts me like a blow every time I meet him. What's going to satisfy him, no matter what pace he should choose to go or how many things he is driven by unhappiness to indulge himself in?

And it was true that everything done up in the town had its effect down in the Settlement. The lodge hall over the Last Chance was the only hall available for the young people in the Settlement to dance, and the bar of the East Chance, at which old Jacob Ensley officiated, was no better stocked than the lockers at the Country Club. And all of us knew that very frequently Billy and Nickols and the rest of our friends went down to dance and drink with the girls from the mills and the shops. Billy had told me once that Milly Burt, who stays at the cigar stand in the Goodloe Hotel in Goodloets, dances so much like me and is so perfumed with my especial sachet from France, Mother Spurlock having collected the chiffon blouse from me for her to wear at the entertainment of the Epworth League, that he came very near addressing her by my name in giving her the invitation to the dance.

"Settlement or Town, they all add up to the sum of girl," he laughed, as he told me about that Saturday night frolic in the Last Chance.

It was the day after Billy's account of the ball at the Last Chance, in which Luella May and Milly and the rest had frolicked in what ought to have been a perfectly harmless way, that Mother Spurlock came to spend the afternoon with me and in which we wrestled until I was almost on the mat - not quite.

"Goodloets has always been the gayest town in the state, but it has now reached the place of the most wicked," she said, after a few preliminary shots had been exchanged. "Every dignity of tradition seems to have been dropped and everybody is dance or play or drink or speed mad. You are the most influential personality in the whole town and I want you to call a halt."

"But aren't they all happy? Isn't everybody getting the most out of life? The men are all working to their capacity and making more money than they ever have before. Why shouldn't they play hard?" I answered her, as I seated myself in the broad window seat of my room opposite the wide maternal ancestral rocker she had chosen.

"Are they happy?" she asked, with her keen eyes on my face.

"They seem to be," I parried.

"Well, as far as personal happiness is concerned I think it is not worth talking about. It is the good of the whole for which I am working, for which I am contending to-day. What you women do, who are not obliged to add to the work of the world that you may live in it, is not of any great importance; it is for the toilers in the vineyard that I plead. The girls and young men in this town cannot dance and drink and play all night and do the constructive work of the community in the daytime. If Luella May Spain falls asleep or nods at her typewriter and fails to get out the telegram to you or Nickols which Mr. Tate has shouted to her off the keys, do you excuse her because she has been fatiguing herself until midnight trying to learn some new dance that Billy Harvey has brought down to the Last Chance from your Country Club? You would not! She would be fired on your complaint."

"But are we responsible for how the girls and men in the Settlement spend their evenings?" I demanded with a fine show of indignation, but with a thrill of fear in my heart. There has always been something in Luella May Spain's shy and admiring glances that drew me and I have always lingered to chat with her a few minutes if business called me into the station. The last time I had spoken to her, not a week before, she had seemed pale and listless and had answered me with indifference.

"You and your class are the ones in power and what you do and what you think is a moral influence that reaches and permeates every soul in this town. You are not about your Father's business; and those less powerful of brain and character follow you in by-paths from the straight road. They are his Little Ones and you lead their feet into brambles. Oh, Charlotte!" And Mother Spurlock stretched out her hands to me in entreaty.

"I'm not a leader," I denied her. "I don't see a foot ahead of me. I'm not worth anything. I'm just living and trying to have a good time doing it. You have got a leader, there over the hedge; why don't they follow him and not me?"

"Before you came Gregory Goodloe had services three times a week at your Country Club, at which the Settlement met the Town. You were not willing that even those few hours should be given over to the learning of the Father's will from one whose mind and soul are ready to teach, and you swept away his pews and his influence. And your dance tunes, to which even I yielded, ring in the ears of his flock to drown out the echoes of God's hymns. And now those who had begun to lean on him and to follow him are turning to persecute him. When Jacob Ensley is drunk he openly charges him with inveigling Martha away and hiding her. He was in a dangerous state one night a week ago and Billy Harvey had to lock him up in his own wine cellar to keep him and a few of his hangers-on from 'going after the parson,' who was down there praying with old Jennie Neil as she died. He doesn't know his danger from Jacob and I think Billy ought to tell him. All Goodloets has admired and aped you since your birth, and now that you discountenance him they are again following you. There were only ten people at prayer meeting last night in the chapel, and the Wednesday before you turned him out of the Club which had offered him its hospitality, there were one hundred and thirty, Settlement and Town about evenly represented. You are responsible for that prayer meeting last night. You may be responsible for the result of one of Jacob's drunken fits. Sometime you'll have to answer for what you do."

"No, Mother Spurlock, I'm not responsible for the failure of Gregory Goodloe to get to the heart of your people and hold them happy to his services and observances, and I'm certainly not responsible for his personal safety. What he offers is not enough to satisfy. His members prefer their Country Club and their Last Chance and their knitting and embroidery. What we all need from the Country Club to the Last Chance is some-thing that makes us want to be constructive, race constructive, so that life will be desirable on through immortality, if there is such a thing. I can't get a glimpse of it. Can you?" and I questioned her beseechingly.

"I can. I do! I have faith in my Father's plan to lead me through 'deep waters' into 'pleasant pastures,'" she answered me, as her eyes looked past me out at Paradise Ridge beyond the chapel.

"Then give it to me," I demanded.

"I can't. You must seek it yourself, and when you get it you will be able to pour it out into the hearts of others as living water. I serve by using my two talents of mercy and love, but God will some day give you ten and you will have to return an hundred fold. He has given the ten to Gregory Goodloe, and now is the night of his despair, but his morning will dawn. You can't dance down and drink down and gamble down and lust down a man like that. He can bide his time until his sheep come to the fold to be fed and warmed in his bosom."

"What practical thing can I do to make you believe that I do not mean to pull down any structure that another human is building up with the hope it is for the good of the whole, Mother Spurlock?" I demanded of her, goaded to the last point of endurance.

"The dedication services of the chapel will be next Sunday. Come, bring Nickols and your father, and let the Town and Settlement see your respect for Mr. Goodloe and for his church," she demanded, as she rose to go, with patient defeat but a lingering hope in her voice and manner.

"Endorse something that means nothing to me?" I asked with pained patience. "You say the people follow me; shall I lead them to drink from a spring that I consider dry, that is dry and has no water for my thirst? No, Mother Spurlock, if the people among whom I have been born trust me I will only lead them by going into paths I know and in which I walk for my own good or pleasure."

"To the Last Chance?"

"At least they get joy there that makes toil easier or offsets the grind," I answered her.

"Is that your final -" she was asking me with her deep, wise old eyes searching me, when she was interrupted by the banging open of my door and the inburst of young Charlotte, young James as ever at her heels, with Sue clinging to his hand. To-day, however, Charlotte had added one to her cohorts, for she led by the hand a very dirty specimen of the masculine gender, somewhat larger than herself and with a flaming red head.

"This is Mikey Burns, Aunt Charlotte, and he's a nice little boy that's dirty and hungry because his mother has got seven like him. Won't you wash him and feed him so we can play with him? The preacher cleaned up four for us to play with yesterday and they are still clean enough. If you clean Mikey I can have a baseball nine, with Sue to get the balls that we don't hit. She gets balls nicely and Mikey throws lots straighter than I can. Jimmy can hit 'em, too, with a wide stick."

"I tan git 'em," declaimed small Sue with great pride.

"I can pitch 'em," also declared Mikey, with evident desire to back up his patroness. "But not as good as her," and his admiration amounted to adoration, as he raised his young eyes to Charlotte.

"You see, Oh, you see, even to the second generation they follow," laughed Mother Spurlock, as she escaped through the door and left me with my practical demonstration of class leadership.

"Wash him, Auntie Charlotte, wash him," Charlotte continued to insist. "I made Jimmy steal some of his things for him while nurse was downstairs. Here they are," and young James, the thief and aforementioned murderer, gave up his stolen goods. "And Mr. Nickols says that all the Settlement children will go to school with us in the nice schoolhouse he and Judge Powers and Minister are going to build in front of Mother Spurlock's orchard. That is a law and then we'll have good times, all of us. There is not many children in the Town and they are all too dressed up, but it is a million down in the Settlement and we are going to have two baseball nines and two armies to battle with. I asked Mr. Nickols to have a place to wash the Settlements and he said he had thought of that and is going to have five shower baths. If you'll just wash Mikey for me I'll help you. I can attend to Jimmy's ears for nurse real good, can't I, Jimmy?"

"Yes," responded Jimmy with brotherly pride.

"No," remonstrated Mikey with abject fear, for the sake of his ears or propriety I was not sure.

I got past the question by motioning him into my bathroom and sending Charlotte and Sue to bring Dabney. Dabney is Charlotte's slave and was soon under way to execute her commands upon Mikey while I beguiled her from the super-intendence thereof down into the garden with me, where from my window I could see Nickols and father in deep conclave over some drawings. Father had discarded his Henry Clay costume and looked young and alive in some of Nickols' flannels and linen. They looked up with interest as I came down the flagstone walk with Charlotte trotting on my one side and wee Sue clinging on the other.

"I'm glad you have come, daughter," said father, as he held up one of the large blue prints before me. "Now you can help Nickols and me locate the exact spot for the public school building. See, here is the public square of Goodloets, with the courthouse in the middle."

"That courthouse is as good as any minor *hotels de ville* in any of the small towns in France," said Nickols, as he came and stood beside me, looking over my shoulder at the map. "The Farmers' Bank and one or two of the very old brick stores are good, too," he added.

"Now, this is Main Street that leads past us down into the Settlement. Here is the Poplars, here the chapel, and this is Elsie Spurlock's house. Nickols and the parson are inclined to place the schoolhouse right opposite, but I am afraid it is too near the Settlement and too far from the Town. Do you suppose the Town children will be able to walk so far?"

"Do you really - really plan to have the Town and the Settlement go to school together?" I gasped.

"Well, Goodloe thinks that the ideal public school system is only to be executed in a democratic -" father was saying, when Nickols interrupted him.

"What does it matter where the two and a half kids from the decadent old families that are dying out go to school? Their sterile parents can motor 'em down to education!" he exclaimed. "Right here is the logical place for the school with the meadow behind it to give a bit of distance, the oak grove back of that, the Country Club beyond, with the river beginning to curve it in. It solidifies and unifies the landscape of the whole town and puts all the community centers where they belong. The Town and Settlement straggled a bit before, but the chapel and the school will unite them! Braid says the schoolhouse can be built of weathered stone and concrete and finished by September fifth, in time to start school. Wilkerson can begin immediately putting out his hedges and the Reverend Gregory is down there now finishing laying out the playground with his ball park."

"That's it - that's the baseball nine Dabney is washing Mikey for!" exclaimed Charlotte, catching up with the conversation. "And when we all go to school with the Settlements and they are clean some, and Mildred Payne and Grace Sproul and some of the others get dirty a little, nobody will know the difference and we can play ball and scouts and everything Minister teaches us. That school makes enough children to do things. We haven't got enough for anything, but the Settlements have, and it is mighty good of them to come up and let us play with them."

"Keep up with the times, Charlotte; don't be a back number. Miss Olymphia Lassiter's school may have held you and Nell, but it will never hold young Charlotte," Nickols jeered, as father began to roll up the map and speak to a young man that the great Wilkerson of White Plains had sent down to juggle with the flora and fauna of the Harpeth Valley.

CHAPTER X

WATER AND OIL

I turned from Nickols' raillery and surveyed the great American garden. The weeks had flown from May to late July and father's plans were beginning to be materialized. Where the sunken garden had been filled in a wide stone well house, the like of which can be found at many of the farmhouses in the Harpeth Valley, had been built and a chain wheel and bucket drew up the water from the deep cistern, which was supplied with underground pipes from the south wing of the Poplars.

"There is no water as soft as open-top cistern water, aerated by a chain and bucket," father had informed me, and he and Dabney consumed buckets of it, while Mammy refused anything else for cooking purposes and insisted on a nightly bath of it for my face. A white clematis in full bloom clambered over the eaves of the low stone house and a blush rose nodded at its door, beside which was placed a rough bench made of square stones and two large slabs, equally moss-covered and worn.

"It is growing to be perfectly wonderful, Nickols," I said, as if I had seen it for the first time, while my eyes followed the sweep of the flagstone walk from the well house beneath the old graybeard poplars out past stretches of velvety lawn, with groups of shrubs and trees casting deep shadows even to the kitchen garden, whose long rows of vegetables, bordered with

Maria Thompson Daviess

old-fashioned blooming herbs and savories, led the observer out into the meadows to the Home Farm and beyond to the dim line of Paradise Ridge. "It is different and distinctive and - and American," I added.

"After this garden and the school are finished and a few of the unfortunate restorations taken away from some of the old houses, like the porch at Mrs. Sproul's and that bathroom addition of Morgan's, I am going to bring Jeffries down in his private car and it will be difficult to keep him from offering to buy Goodloets and have it all shipped up the Hudson. Really, Charlotte, we have seen a vision of the future materialize here and we ought to stand with hats off."

"Whose vision?" I asked, as I stood and let the truth of his statement sink in.

"The parson's spiritual vision perhaps filtering through your father's mentality, which has welded past, present and future. At least, that is the way I see it with the material eye, which is all I have to view it with - if we can call the recognition of beauty and completeness material."

"Now Mikey is nice and clean and we can go to Minister to play, thank you, Aunt Charlotte," at this point young Charlotte broke in to say, thus flinging us a line to haul us out of depths that were slightly over our heads. "Isn't he lovely?" And she gazed upon her new-found comrade with open admiration and self-congratulation.

And small Mikey was indeed a bonny kiddie attired in the very stylish trousers and blouse of small James and shining with Dabney's valeting. His nicely plastered red mop to some extent mitigated the effect of the bare and scratched feet and his rollicking blue eyes over a nose as tip-tilted as Charlotte's own bespoke his delight.

"Anyway, me mother made the togs fer Jim," he asserted with great independence, as he rammed his hands into the diminutive pockets in the trousers.

"Yes, she did, and Auntie Harriet paid her for a present to Jimmy. She sews for us and not for Mikey and her other children, because her husband drinks up his money and our husband don't. Come on, let's go help Minister!" was the shot that Charlotte fired, as she departed down the garden path with her cohorts.

"What about that for democracy?" demanded Nickols, as he and father and I all laughed together.

That night at a dinner party Nell was giving I sat next to the Harpeth Jaguar and talked to him for the first time in many weeks. I had been avoiding him and I didn't mind admitting it to myself. There was something disturbing and puzzling in his serene eyes and free, strong, beautiful body that gave me a queer haunting pain back of my breast. Into my scheme of doing those things in life that give pleasure and not doing those things that give pain he somehow would not fit. He had become as much a part of the social fabric of Goodloets as was I, and he came to our dinner parties, motored with us in his long, gray car and was as happy with us seemingly as he was with that same gray car full of small fry from the Settlement or going about the business of the chapel. The car had always reminded me of his evening clothes, which were straight and simple in line with the black silk vest cut up around the collar buttoned in the back, but which were so fine in texture and perfect in cut and fit that they seemed to be some kind of super clothes that ought to be called by a name of their own, just as the people in the Settlement had decided to call the car the "Chariot" as soon as they had stopped resenting a parson's having it, from finding out how easy were its cushions and how swift its ministrations in time of need.

"Parson's Chariot, quick!" had moaned poor old Mrs. Kelly, when she had slipped on Mrs. Burns' wet doorstep and dislocated her hip. Little Katie Moore had been driven home as swiftly as if on wings after old Dr. Harding had been overtaken, ten miles out on Providence Road, and had used the back seat for an operating table while he put her small splintered ankle in place between splints improvised by a long knife from the car's kit.

And from a distance I had wondered at the Reverend Gregory Goodloe, wondered at his freedom from all resentment because of his ministerial and spiritual failures and at his loving serenity and enjoyment of us all. He partook of the joy in almost all of our adventures in pleasure, and when we did things that in the nature of the case would seem to merit his disapproval, he never administered it; he simply was not with us, but was serenely about his business at the other end of the town from the Country Club or the Last Chance, at whichever resort the entertainment that did not interest him was in progress. He seemed especially to enjoy coming to our dinner parties and he was such a delight with his keen-bladed wit, his flow of joyous laughter and high spirits and the music that bubbled up without accompaniment or denial whenever we asked for it, that not a woman in town would invite the rest to dine until she was sure of securing him first.

"He's so economical," said Nell Morgan, as I helped her arrange her guests for Mark's birthday dinner. While she talked I paused to consider where to put Harriet Henderson and then dropped her card beside Mark's with a little ache in my heart as I tucked Cliff Gray in by Jessie Litton and left the place next Nell vacant for Billy. "People never empty their champagne glasses when Mr. Goodloe gets to talking, and you can put the extra bottles back in the cellar for next time. Do you suppose he does it on purpose?"

"Nobody could be as completely happy as he was at Jessie's Friday night *on purpose*," I answered, as I laid the last card and went with Nell to greet her first guests.

After the soup I turned toward the Reverend Mr. Goodloe, whose card I had placed next my own, and found him looking at me with a particular softness in his eyes under the dull gold.

"Charlotte's and Mikey's nine won twenty-eight to eighteen against Tommy Braidy and Maudie Burns. Thank you for getting the pitcher into his togs," he said, as he squared his shoulders slightly against the rest of the world, the rest of the diners in particular, and bent toward me in just that deferential angle that a man uses when he wants to signal to the others that for a limited time he desires sole possession of the woman dining next to him.

"Your mixing of water and oil in the educational scheme is interesting me greatly," I answered him with a laugh. "Do you really think it will succeed?"

"Any kind of kingdom can be built in the heart of a child, an oligarchy, a democracy or a republic," he answered quickly. "Your name-daughter is a born socialist."

"She and James are murderers and liars and thieves and are wholly engaging. Sue is fast learning from them the habits of their underworld and is asleep upstairs now with Harriet's silver and jade chain, which she brought home with her without the knowledge of the owner this afternoon. What are you going to do about them? I take it you intend to build a kingdom in and of their hearts."

"Weed 'em, like Dabney and I did your dahlia bank ten times at least this spring. You didn't help with the dahlias, but maybe you will with the young Tenderloiners." His eyes entreated mine with a soft radiance that almost made me dizzy.

"I wouldn't know weeds from flowers, 'Minister,'" I answered with prompt denial of his plea, but with a soft use of the children's name for him.

"I don't always know. Let's study botany - together," he again hazarded daringly, and from the tenderness that suddenly curved his strong mouth I knew my soft answer had hit its mark. "Are you coming to the dedication of the chapel a week from Sunday?" He asked me the question directly and with all his softness gone and a commanding note in his voice and direct look. His jeweled eyes were so deep back under their dull gold brows that between the bars of black lashes they looked like stars shining down through a radiant night. They threw their rays directly down into my heart and I could see that their owner was reading the hieroglyphics of my uncertainties and that I could not hide them from him.

"I am not," I answered him with the frankness that his gaze compelled.

"I'll not dedicate it until you help me do it and -" he was saying quietly and positively, when Billy broke in over the excluding shoulder. Billy really adores Gregory Goodloe, but he enjoys going to the limit of his ministerial endurance. Over that limit he has never stepped and he never will; none of them ever will, for there is that in the Harpeth Jaguar which commands the very essence of respect for himself as well as his cloth.

"Say, Parson, what's that about the dedication of the chapel?" he asked, as he twirled his champagne glass to break a few bubbles. "Charlotte and Nickols are going to give Harriet and me that tennis dressing down Sunday week if you don't need us to dedicate with."

"No, I won't need you," answered the Reverend Mr. Goodloe, in an easy agreeable voice, but that had in it the note that he always uses to make Billy halt. "I'm not going to dedicate it yet."

"Why?" came in a perfect chorus.

"I've been working night and day on that altar cloth because I depended on you to know the date of the dedication of your own church. I have danced only once this week," said Letitia Cockrell, with her usual bland directness.

"The communion service from Gorham's has been packed

away unopened in my office a week," Hampton added in an aggrieved voice. "They hurried it for us and it has to be sent back, piece at a time, to be marked."

"The baptismal font is perfectly beautiful and I want the Suckling sprinkled from it first. If you don't hurry she will get old enough to misbehave herself. I know I promised, but I have decided that I can never have the others baptized now, they are too bad," said Nell, as she paused and listened for some sort of explosion from above as she did every minute or two.

"I'll rope Charlotte and drag her to the altar for you, and Mark can sit on her feet while the parson sprinkles," offered Billy, and they all laughed at the picture that he conjured, which seemed to be in keeping with many scenes we had witnessed in the life of small Charlotte.

"That won't be necessary. She will stand before me with folded hands when her time comes," answered Mr. Goodloe, after he had laughed as heartily as anybody else at Billy's threat. "The greatest difficulty will be in persuading her to allow me to conduct my own services."

"But what did you put off the dedication date for?" demanded Letitia, with the hurry over the altar cloth still rankling.

"I put off the dedication of the chapel until all of the people for whom I cared deeply, whose cooperation with me is positively necessary, should be ready to come and help me in the services. When that time comes I will have the dedication. It may be a year and it may be a - day," the parson answered with cool directness.

"If you mean Charlotte, the offer I made for young Charlotte holds good," said Billy with positive glee. "If you want her I'll rope her and drag her in and the rest of you can bid for who holds her down while being branded."

"And my answer to your generous offer, Billy Harvey, is -" Mr. Goodloe paused and looked at me, and Jessie giggled with nervousness - "the same that I made to your offer about the constraining of young Charlotte."

"Still it would be great sport to see both the Charlottes -" Billy was saying, when a servant brought a note on his tray and handed it to Mr. Goodloe, who glanced at it and then hurriedly opened and read it.

"I am sorry, Mrs. Morgan, but will you let me answer this summons?" he asked, and there was the regret in his rich voice of a great boy at being snatched from a feast. "I am so hungry," he added with a laugh.

"Come back later. I'll save some of everything for you," said Nell pleadingly.

"I will if I can," he answered. There was an excited smoulder in the stars under the dull gold that made me restless and my eyes sought and claimed his for a second in which a quick flash of the jeweled tenderness of comprehension was flashed into my depths.

"Good-bye, everybody," he said, and in a second was out of the dining room and we could hear him running down the steps.

"Oh, dear, if he just wasn't a preacher," sighed Harriet. "I suppose somebody in the Settlement is dead or borned or drunk, and he has to go and see about it. I wish -"

"Great Jehovah!" exclaimed Billy, as he suddenly jumped to his feet. "Ensley is fighting drunk and has the gang around the Last Chance. Parson's life isn't worth a tinker's damn if he runs foul of them with all that talk about Martha Ensley and Jacob's threat. She came back last night and Goodloe threatened to have Jacob arrested for beating her. Come on, Nickols, and let's follow him. We'll be enough. The rest of you go on eating, drinking and merrying because old Mark was born. We'll come right back just as soon as we see that all is serene on the Potomac of the Last Chance." And with a last hasty gulp at his wine glass Billy followed Nickols out of the room. Nickols was both white and livid and the expression of his face frightened me, for I knew that Billy would minimize any kind of danger in the presence of a woman while Nickols would not take that trouble.

It was with a queer breathlessness that we all sat before our wine glasses in the midst of the perfume from the rich food and dying flowers and waited - for what we didn't know.

Then it came!

A shot rang out clear and clean in the darkness and was quickly followed by three barking echoes from a repeater.

And there seated in my chair in the brilliantly lighted room, blocks away from the scene, I felt a bullet thud against dull gold.

CHAPTER XI

A BIT OF RAW LIFE

I don't know by what means of personal transportation my body was carried down the street to the public square and to the pavement in front of the courthouse, but I found myself standing there over a woman who had raised Gregory Goodloe's head on her arm and was drawing deep, hard sobs as she held a handkerchief to stanch a flow of blood that showed crimson in the flash from Nickols' electric cigar lighter.

"'When men shall revile you, and persecute you, and say all manner of evil against you falsely for my sake -'" I quoted to myself softly as I stood and looked down on the prostrate figure of the big lithe Harpeth Jaguar while Billy struggled with a man a little way off in the darkness and Nickols shut off the light and went to his aid. I didn't know exactly where the words that rose so suddenly from my heart to my lips had come from, and I only vaguely understood them, but I seemed to be saying them without my own volition.

"Yes, my God, yes, that's what they've done to him," sobbed Martha as she looked up, peering at me through the darkness. "Pa is drunk, Miss Charlotte; and the rest egged him on. This is the only friend I've got and they've killed him."

"Not by a good deal, Martha," came in a hearty grand opera voice just as I dropped on my knee, and in time to stop me from taking that bleeding gold head on my own breast and -

"Jacob's bullet just clipped me but its impact was as good as his fist would have been, which I wish he had used." And as he spoke the wounded parson sprang lithely to his feet and left us two women kneeling before him. In an instant a thought of Mary and the Magdalen flashed through my brain as he bent to raise me to my feet, while Martha crouched away from us in the dark.

"Charlotte?" he questioned softly, as if not willing to believe the witness of his hands and eyes, muffled by the starry darkness.

"Young Charlotte stones you and Jacob shoots you, and I -" I both sobbed and laughed as I clung to his hand just as I heard Billy and Nickols throw the cursing, panting man to the ground not ten feet away.

"Now then, Parson, we've got Jacob down and out. Nickols has got his foot on his neck and I've got his pistol. What do you want done with him?" Billy interrupted me pantingly to demand.

"Let him up," answered Mr. Goodloe, as he gently extricated himself from my clinging hand and went over to the scene of the conflict. "Had enough, Jacob?" he asked just as gently as he had unhanded himself from me.

"I'll have had enough when I put you where you can't entice my girl again," answered Jacob as he rose slowly to his feet. As he spoke Billy went and stood beside the parson and Nickols stepped behind them into the shadow in which Martha crouched.

"You know that is not true, Jacob. I helped Martha to go away to a place of safety to earn her living and keep her honesty. Isn't that so, Martha?" the rich voice softly asked the woman crouching in the dark.

"I told him that but he wouldn't believe me and the others

don't," she answered with a sob that was almost a shudder of fear.

"What did she come back fer then?" demanded Jacob. "Answer me that. And didn't she go straight to your preaching and praying joint like all the other women, fine and sluts, do?" The liquor was still burning in Jacob's head but at those words he got a response from the impact of Billy's fist that again laid him low.

"Oh, I dasn't say nothing. I dasn't," moaned Martha, as she clutched at my skirts just as Nell and Hampton began to arrive on the scene of action, followed by Harriet and Mark and the others. They were all panting and wild with anxiety. They had taken the wrong turning at the end of the square and had gone around the block, thus giving the little tragedy time to enact itself before a mercifully small audience.

"Go away quickly, Martha, in the shadow," I bent and whispered to the trembling woman, and I didn't know where the sympathy in my voice came from as I stood between her and the rest while she slipped behind an old horse block before the court house gate and off in the darkness towards the Settlement before they had noticed her presence.

"Anybody hurt? What's the matter?" gasped Mark as he seized hold of the Reverend Mr. Goodloe's arm.

"Nothing serious," answered the parson in a voice that calmed the others like oil on choppy water. "Jacob Ensley is out on a drunk and Billy had to knock him down to quiet him. All of you go back to dinner quickly, for I don't see why Sergeant Rogers should get Jacob this time. Billy will help me get him home and I'll remonstrate with him when he is sober. I'd rather do it at the Last Chance than at the jail. Jacob is a leading citizen and I don't want a jail smirch on him. I intend to use him later. Now all of you go. Go!" His voice was as gently positive as if he had been speaking to a lot of children and nobody seemed even to think of rebelling but we all began to fade away into the starlight as rapidly as we had assembled and more quietly.

"Thank you, and bless you," he said to me, as I went past him in the darkness, and for just a second I suspected that his hand was laid on my black braids but I was not sure. I knew the gratitude was for my getting Martha off the scene of action so quietly and swiftly.

"A bit of raw life for you, Charlotte," Nickols remarked as he went with me through the fragrant night back to Mark's and Nell's feast. "The eternal girl, two-men melee."

"In this case it was girl - three men, the third skunking it," I answered in words as coarse and as forcible as the scene I had just witnessed. "I'd like to get my bare hands around the throat of the man who is hiding behind Martha and that little child."

"That remark from you, my dear Charlotte, just goes to show that when women get even the smell of bloodshed they become fiercer than the male," said Nickols with a cool laugh that further infuriated me.

"Yes, I do feel like a female jaguar," I answered hotly and then collapsed inside at the use of that name for myself in conjunction with my secret title for the Reverend Mr. Goodloe.

"It would be better if you felt yourself in the character of a ferret if you intend to go out on a still hunt for all unacknowledged paternity, even in dear, simple, little old Goodloets," Nickols further jeered as we came up the steps of the Morgan house from where the others were just going into the dining room to resume their eating and drinking and being merry.

"I'll find that one man," I answered as I swept into the dining room, seated myself in my place and drained my glass of flat wine.

"Heaven help him!" laughed Nickols wickedly, and he raised

Mr. Goodloe's full glass as he slipped into his place beside me.

For a week after the shooting fray my soul sulked darkly in its tent and meditated while I went on my usual gay rounds of self-enjoyment. The garden was being brought to a most glorious mid-August triumph and the inhabitants for miles around were coming to see it. All of father's old friends, from whom he had shrunk in the last years, hung around him in the old way. He sat with them under the old graybeard poplars around which had been planted a plantation of slim young larches by the wizard of White Plains. From discussions about gardening and Americanisms all the old Solons of the local bar, and even of the towns around, gradually led their fallen leader back into his place and were battling with him over politics and jurisprudence as they had in past days. The day I went into his library to ask father about employing another likely black garden boy that Dabney had discovered, and found him, Judge Monfort from over at Hillcrest in the third district, Mr. Cockrell and Mr. Sproul around his table deep in huge volumes from the shelves, buried in a cloud of tobacco smoke and argument in which Latin words flew back and forth, I went up to my room and stood helpless before my window looking out towards Paradise Ridge.

"I want to thank somebody and there is nobody to thank," I whispered, with a great emptiness within me. That was the bitterest cry of need my heart had ever given forth, and I went swiftly down to Nickols in the garden and told him what I had seen and heard.

"It really is a remarkable come-back, sweetheart," he said, with the most exquisite sympathy in his voice and face. "Mark Morgan told me just an hour ago that they want to have him appointed back to his old place on the bench and Mr. Cockrell answered the President's inquiry for a man from this section for the Commerce Commission with the judge's name. It'll be great to see the old boy on one of the seats of the mighty again, thanks to the sweat of his brow and mind in this village manifestation of American nationalism which has grown out of our little old garden plan."

"What can a man or woman do to render gratitude if there seems to be nobody to take it, Nickols?" I asked him, not expecting, as usual, that he would understand me. For once he did.

"The philosophies all teach 'hand it on' in that case," he answered me.

"I'll hand it on to Martha Ensley and help her and her child to their place under the sun," I said slowly, thus by having a reason and an obligation back of it, ratifying the vow I had already taken.

"That is an impossibility," answered Nickols with easy coolness. "The one 'come-back' that is impossible is the woman in that kind of a situation."

"I'll never admit such an injustice as that," I said, and I had a queer premonition that I would be held to that declaration.

The very next morning after my declaration of purpose to "hand on" my father's "come-back" I went down into the Settlement to hunt for Martha Ensley, not that I was really suffering about her, but because I felt a kind of obligation to begin at once a thing that it appealed to my sense of justice to accomplish.

Sometimes in mid-August there comes down a night over the hot, lush, maturing Harpeth Valley which is like a benediction that sprinkles cool dew on a thirsting heart. And now the morning was cool and brilliant, with the sun evaporating the heavy dew in soft clouds of perfume from the grain fields, the meadows and the upturned soil out where the farmers were breaking ground after the first harvests. I felt strong and calm and full of an electric energy, which I found I needed before I had more than started my quest.

I put on my tennis clothes, snowy from collar to shoe tips, like the trappings of the White Knight, and started to walk down into the Settlement to find Martha. I intended to stop at Mother Spurlock's "Little House Beside the Road," and some vague idea was in my mind of having her dispatch a messenger to summons Martha to the interview I was about to bestow upon her. That is not the way it all happened and I was hot and dusty and sweat-drenched before I had been on my quest more than a few hours.

Mother Elsie was not at home. The door to the Little House was wide open, as it always is when cold or rain does not close it, and huge old Tabby with one eye purred on the doorstep in the sun. A bird was nesting in the wisteria vine above the door and her soft whirring bespoke an interesting domestic event as near at hand. It did not in the least disturb Tab, and I wondered at the harmony between traditional enemies that I met on Mother Spurlock's very doorstep. I went in and drew myself a drink of fresh cool water from the cistern at the back door, looked in a tin box over the kitchen table and took three crisp tea cakes therefrom. I picked up a half knitted sock from beside the huge split rocker in the shade of the gnarled old apple tree, which was a rooftree in every sense of the word, for it crowded close against the door and hovered in the whole tiny house. Just before I left I put all the loose change I had in my white linen skirt pocket in an old lacquered tea canister which had a slit in it cut with a can opener, and that stood on the shelf of the old rock chimney in the low living room. I had never heard that canister mentioned by Mother Spurlock and I don't know how I knew that out of it came the emergency funds for many a crisis in the Settlement. Then last I picked a blush rose from the monthly bloomer trailing up and over the window and laid it on the empty, worn old Bible on the wide arm of the rocker beside a pair of horn-rimmed spectacles. Then I hesitated. I had been so sure of finding Mother Spurlock at home and having her hunt up Martha for me that I found it difficult to adjust myself to my first complexity of plans. And while I hesitated a resolve came into my mind with the completeness of a spoken direction.

"She lives at the Last Chance and I'll go right down there and find her," I said to myself, as I started along the peony-bordered path to the front gate of the Little House, over which a huge late snowball was drooping, loaded down with snowy balls that would hold their own until almost the time for frost. At my own decision I had a delicious little feeling of fear, which was at least justifiable when I thought of that huge drunken figure wrestling with Billy in the darkness and whom I knew to be the proprietor of the resort into which I had determined to penetrate. Also, from my early youth I had heard Jacob Ensley and the Last Chance spoken of in tones of dread disapproval. Before I should become really frightened I hurried down the hill, past the squalid and tumble-down mill cottages which I had never really seen before, where it seemed to me millions of children swarmed in and around and about, and at last arrived at the infamous social center of the Settlement.

And my astonishment was profound to find that the Last Chance sign hung over a very prosperous grocery with boxes and barrels of provender out on the pavement under an awning and with huge, newly-painted screen doors guarding the wide entrance, at which I hesitated.

"Come right in, lady, come right in," called a cheerful, booming man's voice, and the door was swung open by a large man in a white apron, with blue eyes that crinkled at the corners, a wide smile and white hair. "What can we do for you to-day? We've a nice lot of late dewberries just in from over on Paradise Ridge."

"I'm - I'm looking for the - the Last Chance Saloon," I faltered, because I was too astonished to utter anything but the truth to the delightful and tenderly solicitous man standing before me in his huge, clean white apron over his blue shirt that matched his eyes.

"Well, lady," the nice Irish voice faltered a trifle, about as mine had, though plainly with controlled astonishment tinged with

Maria Thompson Daviess

amusement, "could I get you anything to - to cool you off and bring it out here in the grocery? It is cooler than it is back at the bar. I said to myself jest last week, so I did, I said to myself, 'Jacob, you ought to get a sody-water fountain for the ladies what has the same right to thirst as a man.' And I will, too, if my bad luck just leaves me. How about a nice cool bottle of beer sitting comfortable here before the counter?"

"Are you - *you* - Jacob - I mean - Mr. Jacob Ensley?" I further gasped. This daylight materialization of the grewsome beast of the night was too much for me.

"Jacob Ensley at your service, Miss," he answered with easy dignity. "Now, will it be the bottle of beer I shall bring you? Or there's a new drink I might mix fer you that a young gentleman friend of mine from New York has taught me, and with a good Irish name of Thomas Collins - the drink, not the young gentleman." Nickols had been living on Tom Collins for the last month and I instantly knew that I recognized the young friend from New York. Also my wits were at a branching of the road and I didn't know just what to do or say as Jacob waited with easy courtesy for my decision. And again I was too much perturbed for invention and had to speak out the truth.

"I'm Charlotte Powers, Mr. Ensley, and I came down to see your daughter, Martha," I said, looking directly into his clear friendly eyes which I saw instantly darken with a storm as the smile left his nice mouth and it hardened into a straight line.

"I'm sorry, Miss Powers, but my Martha ain't at home right now to you, and I don't know when she will be. Is that all I can do for you? These berries now, from over at Paradise Ridge?" And with the ease of a man of the great upper world Jacob Ensley of the lower walks of life put me out of the door of his private life into the ranks of the meddler and shut it in my face. I acknowledged to myself that my rebuff was justifiable and I was about to make an exit from the scene as gracefully as possible with a box of the really delicious berries under my arm when a cry of terror in a child's voice came from somewhere at the back of the grocery and together the grocer and I ran to see what the matter could be. And at the heels of the proprietor I then penetrated the blind of the grocery and entered the Last Chance.

CHAPTER XII

THE TENACIOUS TURTLE

"It's Martha's Stray," the big man gasped in a kind of impatient alarm. "I just left him here a minute ago to go front." Together he and I started around the long room with its bar on the one side backed up by a mirror whose gilt frame was swathed in mosquito netting and on either side of which were shelves bearing pyramids of bottles. On the bar at one end were piled oranges and at the other lemons and limes whose sophistication seemed out of place somehow in the Settlement in the Harpeth Valley. All the trappings that I judge would go with the dispensing of liquor were present, but our eyes could discover no small child and we stood together and waited anxiously.

"He's got me toe, me toe, and won't let go. He's chewing it off!" at last came a lusty yell from just outside a back door that led out into a side yard from behind the bar, and with one accord the proprietor of the Last Chance and I ran to the scene of the devouring. And as we ran I heard a door slam in the rooms back of the bar and we met Martha face to face on the scene of action. I shall never forget the picture that confronted me there in that little back yard upon which the bar of the Last Chance opened, and I somehow never want to.

On a little grass plot a small boy danced and yelled and firmly to one of the capering feet was hung a large mud turtle which was flapped this way and that by the strenuous young leg, but which held on with apparently every intention of letting only the traditional thunder loosen its grasp on the pink prize.

"Stand still, you Stray, and let me get at the varmint," commanded Jacob impatiently.

"Let mother get the beast, sonny," Martha pleaded as she knelt on the grass and caught the dancing boy by his arm and brought his dervish gyrations to a halt.

I stood unconscious of intrusion and absorbed with interest and watched the operations begun on the tenacious turtle and the writhing toe. Neither of the three principals in the action noticed me at all as Martha held the boy and Jacob bent and took hold of the turtle in his hard brown spotted shell. And as the operations for his liberation were begun the small boy became both still and quiet and I was able to get a good view of him as he leaned against his mother's shoulder and held out the foot to Jacob.

As I looked at him something queer stirred in me with a sharp pain and then was quiet. He was the most delicious bit of five-year-old humanity I had ever beheld and I doubt if any childless woman could have seen such a child cuddle to another woman's breast and shoulder and not have had something of the same thrill of pain. His whiteness and pinkness and sturdy chubbiness were like many another infant's charms but his jet black top-knot that ascended on one side and cascaded over his ear on the other in a hauntingly familiar way, his violet eyes under their long lashes and his clear-cut, firm, commanding mouth, that curled into the bud of a rose as he sobbed and then unfolded into lines of beauty and strength as he hushed at his mother's comforting, were not like any other young human that I had ever beheld.

"It hurts. It hurts!" he sobbed.

"Hush, *you* mustn't cry!" commanded Martha, and there was a little bitter emphasis on the "you" that cut me, I didn't exactly know why.

And immediately the curled mouth was set in a firm line and the long lashes winked back tears.

"The beast will not leave go at all," was Jacob's verdict as after a careful twisting and turning of the ugly turtle he rose to his feet. "And they do say to kill it lets a venom into the place it is holt of. I dunno what to do." And in his uncertainty Jacob's eyes sought my face while at the same instant Martha lifted her wistful eyes to mine. It was the instinctive turning of the masses to the domination of my class in the time of need of leadership.

"You git it, lady," suddenly demanded the kiddie, and in his voice and glance there was none of the deferring to a superior force that I felt in the others but a decided command of that force. And as he spoke he stretched out an imperious hand that caught and clung to mine. "Git down and git it," he again commanded.

"Have you any ammonia, Martha?" I asked, my wits responding gallantly to the sudden demand upon their biological knowledge.

"I've some in the chist behind the bar. Times I uses it strong on heavy drunks," responded Jacob and he went quickly into the bar and returned with the bottle. "It's customers in the grocery and customers at the bar that I'm keeping waiting fooling along with the brat and the varmint," he grumbled.

"I can manage the turtle and you can go and attend to the customers," I answered, thus assuming calmly the command of the craft of the Last Chance. Jacob immediately took me at my word and disappeared into the bar.

"Let's take him and lay him on the bed so we can muffle the turtle in a towel while we use the ammonia," I said to Martha.

"Yes," answered Martha, "that will be best. Let mother carry you, sonny!" and Martha bent as if to lift him in her arms.

"I kin hop," the young sufferer announced. "I'm too big to carry, I am," he added with proud consideration in his glance at Martha's frailness.

"I'll carry you and mother can carry the turtle," I answered, and to prevent further delay I lifted him in my strong arms while Martha took the turtle in her hands, protected by the gingham apron that she wore. The black head wilted against my breast and the serious young violet eyes were raised to mine in frightened confidence.

"It's a mighty big turkle," he faltered and snuggled closer.

"We'll get him," I reassured, as I laid him on a bed in a room that opened, as did the bar, out on the tiny yard.

And as I had promised we performed upon that stubborn turtle. With a convulsion, as the ammonia fumes entered his nostrils, if he had such things, he let go of the toe, shuddered and withdrew into his shell, to die, I supposed, though I afterwards learned that he crawled off in the night, much to the kiddie's grief.

"That's a bad smell, poor old turkle," was all the thanks I got as the sufferer climbed down from the bed and proceeded to seize his late enemy in intrepid and sympathetic hands. His mother rescued both him and the turtle by placing the latter in a bucket on a table at the window and giving the rescued another bucket to get me a drink of water from the well in the yard.

"Northeast, bottom corner," he promised me with hospitality shining from his entire face as he experimentally hopped out into the yard, then forgot me and the water entirely in making the acquaintance of a very dirty little dog that was barking at him through the fence.

"Oh, he's lovely, Martha," I said, speaking from pure impulse in a way that could not fail to carry conviction and melt the heart of any woman who possessed a treasure like that.

"I know he is, Miss Charlotte," Martha answered with gentle bitterness, "and that makes it all the worse for him."

"It doesn't; it can't be worse for anybody to be born as beautiful and strong as that boy is," I answered her and felt somehow I had fallen head foremost into my mission. "I came down here to see you, Martha, and now that I have seen him - I - it's - it's a shame, all of it," I ended by faltering with a total lack of the eloquence that I felt.

"Yes, it's just that - a shame," Martha admitted to me with a great hopelessness in her black eyes. "And nothing can make it better."

"Something can be done!" I answered hotly. "You are young, Martha, and he's a baby. You can get out of it all and you can get him out and begin all over. I - I'll help you." And as I spoke I took her hand in mine. Mine was brown and hard from tennis and Martha's from toil, but they met and clung.

"I - I tried that, Miss Charlotte. I had to come back," answered Martha, and a bitter passion suddenly lit her pale face. "I'm too young to be let go - yet."

"What do you mean, Martha?" I asked, and suddenly I felt that some kind of chasm had yawned at my feet that I had never suspected to exist before.

"Don't ask me, Miss Charlotte," Martha answered as the passion died out of her face and voice and the sorrow fell over her like a shadow.

"Do you remember that afternoon at Mother Spurlock's when we were ten, and you climbed the tree and got the apples, while I picked them up for her to make apple turn-overs for us?" I asked her suddenly as I held on to her hand when she tried to draw it from me. "I cried for a week to go and see you, Martha, and it was all wrong that I wasn't allowed. My mother would have let me come if she had been alive, but Mammy was an ignorant negro and didn't understand."

"I cried for you, too," answered Martha, as the saddest smile I had ever seen came across the darkness of her face. "And when you was a young lady I crept up to the south window of the Poplars and saw you in your dress for the big coming-out party. You were like an angel from Heaven and I loved you. I wanted to be like you. All us girls did. They have always envied you and watched you, but I loved you. I did! I did, but - what chanct has a girl like me got against a man who's like - like you are? But I did love you; I did!"

"It doesn't seem right to - to either of us to have kept us apart," I faltered, as Martha suddenly slipped to the floor at my feet and put her head in her hands.

"Don't be kind to me - I can't stand that. You mustn't, you mustn't! You wouldn't if you knew," she sobbed.

"I *am* going to be - that is, I *am* going to help you, Martha, and you have got to show me how," I answered her as a kind of determination that was stronger than any like emotion I had ever had came over me. "Tell me what to do, Martha, for you and - and for the kiddie," I commanded her with my usual imperiousness.

"Miss Charlotte," said Martha, as she suddenly rose to her knees, looked up into my face and bared her shoulder with one motion of her hand, "that black bruise is from the licks father gave me when I wouldn't tell him why it was I came back after I went away and why it was I went. He beat me three times to make me tell whose that boy is - when he wasn't a month old. He knew that Mr. Goodloe helped me to go away three months ago and - and begin again, and he don't really believe that the parson enticed me back. The gang just put that in his head when he was drinking. He does think that Mr. Goodloe knows about it all and I'm afraid - afraid that some time when he's drunk he'll try to make him tell and - and - there'll be murder, maybe double murder. I can't tell you anything. I'm a fly caught in a web and I'm being drawn down to hell. I thought there was a way out; the parson prayed with me and I saw it. I saw myself right and honest again, but - but at a word I - I came back. Even the good of the child couldn't hold me when the - the calling came. Please go and leave me, and forget about me and - and don't come down here again."

"No, Martha, I must help you," I answered, decidedly. I had never been able to bear any kind of frustration and this made me doubly determined.

"It's too late, Miss Charlotte, but, Oh, it ain't too late for some of the others. Luella May and Sadie Todd and the rest. Miss Charlotte, make the Town men let 'em alone, and stop the Saturday night games and dances down here. You can do it. Pa would kill me for saying it, for it is then he makes his money, but it isn't fair, it isn't fair. You Town women do the same things, but you are protected and looked after. When Grace Payne gets drunk at your Country Club you take her home yourself and see no harm comes to her, and the men she's with protect her from themselves, but it's not the same with Luella May Spain and - and me."

"How did you know about Grace, Martha?" I faltered with terror in my heart. I felt a kind of class nakedness that made me burn with positive physical shame.

"They all watch and talk about what you do, Miss Charlotte, you especially, because you are more beautiful and more - more strong than the rest. They all said you'd smash our going to the church meetings with the Town folks at the Country Club when you got home. But I always stand up that you are right and you are. The Town on the hill and the Settlement in the valley are better - better apart. That's why I'm begging you to go and leave me to fight it out or go under. Please go!"

"Oh, but, Martha, I didn't - I don't -" I was beginning to falter a denial to what had suddenly struck me as a truth when we were interrupted by the advent of Martha's child, the Stray, as I afterwards found was the only name he possessed, one cruelly indicative of his relation to the social structure of the world into which he had involuntarily been born.

"Bottom of the well, northeast corner," he said, as he set a bucket of water at my feet with a jolt that dashed a small wave over my white buckskins, and he held out a dipper full to me with a little twirling motion that sent another wave on my skirt and which had an unmistakably professional knack to it. I have seen old Wilks set down beer steins and cocktail glasses with exactly that twirl ever since he has officiated at the lockers and sideboard at the Club, and I now know that his motions had the latest Last Chance style to them. Thus, by gossamer links and steel cable, the Town and the Settlement seemed to be held together.

"Excuse me for spilling the water on you," added the young scion of the bartender with grave courtesy, as he held a very dirty little paddie under the drip of the dipper and elevated the drink for me in such a way that I had to steady the small hand that held the handle with mine as I drank.

"Oh, son, how careless!" Martha was just exclaiming when a call in Jacob's sharp voice interrupted her.

"Martha, grocery!" it commanded her and I was not sure whether he was ignorant of the fact that I was still her caller or was interrupting her on purpose. I think Martha shared the same uncertainty; she blushed and looked both ashamed and frightened.

"I'll go now, Martha, out this door that leads onto the street," I hastened to say to relieve her of the dilemma. "But I'm coming back to you," I added with determination, as I made ready to slip out the side door of the Last Chance in regular underworld style.

"Please don't, Miss Charlotte," she called, as she was passing through the other door into the world from which I was escaping. The sad significance of our two exits struck me so forcibly that I was two blocks away before I really became conscious of things around me, and then I was brought back to the squalid street of the Settlement and its surroundings by feeling a damp little hand slipped into mine as I strode along.

"Please take me with you, Miss Lady," the Stray pleaded, as he ran along beside me, trying to keep up with my long steps. "I've got me a dog now to keep off turkles from me and you." And the slinking brindle bunch of ears and tail and very little else, at our heels, regarded me with the same brave entreaty. He and the Stray, indeed, presented a picture of chivalrous attention as they stood regarding me.

"But what will your mother say?" I asked of my small human attendant with conscientious contention against my desire to take them both with me on out of the dirt and heat and flies and other swarming young humans up into the coolness and shade and - loneliness - of my own life.

"She groceries all day and has to forget me," he answered calmly. "You can bring me back to bed when she is through." And to this plea was added a pathetic wag of the brindle tail.

"Well, I'll take you up as far as Mother Spurlock's and give you both a tea cake," I capitulated as I started again up the street of the Settlement towards the haven of the Town.

And as my escort and I progressed through the Settlement I could see the most violent signs of interest being manifested in all of us. Dirty, sweaty women, with their sleeves rolled up, came to the doors to look at us, and as I greeted them one and all with a nod they smiled back with pleased astonishment. I had never been down in the Settlement before, but most of them spoke to me by name and one toothless old woman hastily broke off a bloom from a struggling geranium, came to her rickety gate and offered it to me with an admiring smile.

"Bless my soul, Miss Charlotte, be you a-kidnappin' Martha's Stray?" she asked, as I accepted it with enthusiasm.

"He and the dog are kidnapping me as far as Mother Spurlock's, and then they'll let me go and come back," I answered, with a laugh, as we started on. Not once had the strong little fingers let go of my hand as we stood and talked and they only held the closer as we started climbing the long, hot dusty hill to the Little House by the Side of the Road. But in the long climb not once did the sturdy little legs lag or the small arm drag on my strength. The clasp was one of equality and affectionate attraction, not of dependence.

Maria Thompson Daviess

CHAPTER XIII

THE SHORT-CIRCUIT

And at last we arrived at the old snowball guarding the open
gate of the Little House and we went under its low boughs and
up the walk. But we did not march to an undisputed and
stealthy raid on the tea cake box above the kitchen table. The
Little House was no longer the deserted scene I had left it, but
was teeming with human and juvenile activities which
streamed out to meet us at the door.

"You can't come in here, Auntie Charlotte," was the command
that greeted me at the very doorstep as young Charlotte faced
me with short skirts outspread determinedly, while behind her
Mikey of the red head, Jimmy, Sue, Maudie, the sister of
Mikey, and other known and unknown juveniles, presented a
solid support of defiance. "We are doing some Lord's work
and we don't need you, but we'll let the nice little boy and the
lovely dog come in. We do need them. Come in, little boy!"
and as she spoke Charlotte held out a welcoming hand to the
Stray, who faltered and looked up into my face to see if he
might accept the invitation which evidently swayed him by its
commanding tone.

"Couldn't I come in for just a second?" I asked with all due
meekness.

"Not for even a second," answered Charlotte sternly. "You'd
interrupt Minister. You go away and leave the boy."

"Then how'll I get him back to his mother?" I pleaded, but as I spoke I allowed the little fingers to slip from mine and I pushed the waif towards Charlotte with the greatest confidence, which evidently communicated itself to both him and the dog, for they left me simultaneously and went towards the enemy's camp.

"Shoo, it's only little Stray Ensley. I'll take him home when I go," the redoubtable Mikey assured me with a wide smile at the kiddie, which was answered with a rapture of hero worship.

"What's his name?" demanded Charlotte as if seeking a passport.

"Just Stray," answered Mikey in a matter-of-fact tone of voice. "He ain't got no father, dead or alive."

"Then Stray is just short for stranger, because everybody else has fathers, dead, alive or drunk," said Charlotte, in the same matter-of-fact tone that Mikey had used, and he in no way seemed to feel her remark personally derogatory to his paternal parent.

"Well, let's take him to Minister to be learned his verses of the song and dance. Come on, for we are keeping him and the Lord waiting," said Charlotte as she marshaled them all into the Little House and calmly shut the door in my face and left me standing alone in the middle of the walk. Even the yellow pup had squeezed into the door before it was shut and only I was left in the outer darkness away from the grand opera voice that I could hear booming with a juvenile chorus out at the back of the cottage where I knew the rehearsal was being held under the twin of the old apple tree from which the front roof tree over my head was eternally separated by the Little House. With actual sadness and a queer feeling of shut-outness I did the only thing left to me and sauntered slowly on up the hill under the tall old elm trees that the Town had planted a century ago to keep the heat from the heads of the like of me while the toilers down in the Settlement had no such proof of ancestral care.

"They are producing in the sweat of their brows while I - saunter," I said to myself, as I stretched out my bare arm from which the white silk sleeve had been rolled away after the prevailing mode of the sport for which it was designed, and flexed and regarded the bunch of muscles that knotted themselves on my smooth, tanned forearm.

"It *could* swing a wash tub as well as the best racquet this side of the Meadowbrook Club," I added aloud with a queer kind of primitive shame mixed with my physical pride in myself.

"Or juggle a heavy baby and a kitchen stove into a square meal?" added a laughing voice as the Jaguar padded up beside my shoulder on his tennis shoes before I had heard him at all, so deep was my absorption in my own judgment and absolution of myself.

"Still I was put out just a few minutes ago by a woman half my size," I laughed in return as the long strides shortened into harmony with mine.

"I heard about it and ran after you to ask you to come back or, if you refused, to let me go with you wherever you are going. I left Mother Spurlock in charge of the newly installed Epworth Leaguers. Charlotte disapproved of my coming and said so," and we both laughed in delight over my strenuous name-daughter.

"Are you asking me *quo vadis?*" I demanded, with a look at him out of a corner of my eye that got in return a glint of the jewels under dull gold that always infuriated as well as interested me.

"'Whither thou goest, I will go, and where thou lodgest I will lodge - " the parson suddenly chanted under his breath, using the old Gregorian measure for the few words of the oldest song of impersonal love extant. "Thank you for bringing Martha's boy up to the Little House. Jacob has refused both Mother Spurlock and me to let him come."

"I didn't bring him. He and the pup brought me and then he was stolen from me into the fold, as it were," I answered as I paused at the front gate of the Poplars, which had a white clematis drifting over its tall stone pillars and clutching at the straight iron bars as if trying to keep me out of even my own fold. "Will you come in with me?" I asked with a laugh, as I flung the old gate wide in spite of the tendril fingers.

The parson laughed, whistled a strain of his "whither thou goest" chant to me and followed me across the lawn to the foot of the poplars. On the bench surrounding their trunks I found my basket with the fine seam I was sewing for the Suckling in it and I dropped upon the thick mat of grass on the very edge of the shadow from the silver branches above and began to hunt for my thimble, leaving the Jaguar standing over me.

"Stop looking down on me and come tell me what particular religious incantations were going on from which Charlotte so violently barred me," I laughed up at him, as I threw a flat grass cushion a little way from my skirts, upon which he immediately sank and seemed to curl up at my feet.

"I had the whole bunch rehearsing the children's part in the dedication services of our chapel. Do you know that small Sue can really sing? The rest stagger well but Susan sings. It is delicious. It is going to be hard on you women folks to hear her chant her responses to me on that great day." And as he spoke he looked beyond me over to his beautiful shimmering gray chapel and there was not a glint in his eyes that showed me he was trying to sound out my intentions about attendance on that ceremony.

"Please, Mr. Goodloe, don't be serious in saying as you did last night that you are not going to dedicate your chapel until I - I help you," in all gentleness I said.

"I can't do it until you come," he answered me with just as great gentleness and he turned his head away from me, but not before I saw a glow in his eyes that made me suddenly strong and calm and curiously humble.

"I - I could go as your guest," I faltered, offering a compromise which I felt sure would not be accepted.

"I can't, I just can't dedicate the chapel until you echo my ceremony in your heart," he answered me with his eyes still turned away from me and looking with the greatest sadness out on Paradise Ridge.

"Why?" I asked with a simple directness that the situation demanded and with no trace of the coquetry the question might have held.

"Shall I tell you all of the reason with no reservations?" the parson asked, as he swung around on his mat and faced me, with his eyes looking straight into mine.

"All," I answered.

"In every community there is one soul which holds the real leadership of the souls of those surrounding them. God seems to appoint captains of the regiments of His people to lead them along the way, Christ the captain of all the hosts. Spiritually you are more evolved than any other person in this town and with you doubting I cannot get the others to see. You are so gorgeous and so brilliant that you blind them all. They have always followed your lead - up or down. There are a few like Mother Spurlock who have gained their Christ knowledge through suffering, but they are not of the calibre to help others to gain theirs. With your hand in mine I can make this whole community see and know; separated from you, you going one way and I another, I can do nothing. You simply short-circuit my force and I am helpless without you." He spoke very simply and directly down into my heart.

"That is not true; no one person is responsible for any spiritual decision that another makes," I answered hotly with an awful sense of having had a burden placed on my shoulders that they could not carry.

"The old 'brother's keeper' question will never be settled in any but the right way," he answered me straight from the shoulder. "You are responsible for the attitude of this whole town towards the cause I represent and they'll have to wait for your eyes to be opened and for you to make them see."

"You minimize yourself," I answered quickly, for in some curious way it hurt me to see that great strong man sit at my feet baffled by a force that he declared to be in me but which I did not acknowledge or understand.

"They were listening to me - from a distance, as it were - and I might have made them hear if you had not come home and thrown them back into the old pleasant groove of non-action and non-belief. In a week you had swept away all I had builded in six months." He spoke with simple conviction and not a trace of the bitterness that might have been in the arraignment.

"Everybody in this town adores you," were the words that gushed out of my heart for his comforting before I could stop them. "That is one reason I have acted as I have. I do not, I cannot believe that the religion which is great enough to bring the redemption of the whole race into a desirable immortality can be composed of nine-tenths emotion, with which all of them were following your beautiful voice and beautiful eyes and beautiful church and beautiful words. If I am to be saved it will be by something sterner than that; it will be something that makes me sweat drops of blood from my mind, take up a hard cross of duty and work, work to make the fibre of my soul strong enough to enjoy the robust kind of immortality that alone seems worth while to me. Your Son of Man walked from town to town in the hot sun and taught the people, healed the multitude and yet had not where to lay his head to rest. His church has lost His vigor. Your whole scheme hasn't

Maria Thompson Daviess

enough action in it. Your organization is too easy and too full of surface observances. It is conducted with slipshod business methods and there is no force in it to help me. If I join any church ever it will have to be a new one that can compare with modern business in its efficiency. Your scheme ofredemption to immortality through an efficient mediation is perfectly sound, but you don't back it up."

"The Church of Christ has stood, endured and done business for almost two thousand years," he answered quietly. "It is in some ways all you say of it, but it has at least proved its vitality. Why seek to found a new organization with a new head and a new scheme of immortality if you recognize this scheme as good? The place to reorganize a business is from the inside, not the outside. These people *must* get their vision *now*. Will you come and help me?" As he spoke he looked again down into the depths from which I had been trying to translate some of the hieroglyphics to him and he held out his long powerful hand to me in an entreaty that shook my very foundations.

"You make me want to do as you ask me, but I do not see what it is we should strive for, what it is from which we should be saved. There are tears in my eyes but do you want my emotions without my reason?" And I asked my question with a quiver almost of timidity.

"No, both!" he answered me, as he dropped his hand and arm from their attitude of entreaty, shook his head sadly and again turned from me and looked out on the dim distance of Old Harpeth. Suddenly I had the feeling of having a great door shut in my face, and a terror of being left all alone in the world came over me. Without knowing what I did I stretched out my hand and caught at his arm and moved closer to him, suddenly cold in the sunshine.

"I'm frightened," I whispered, as I bowed my head on my hand, clutching his arm.

"Poor little wandering, hunting lamb," he crooned to me as he laid a tender hand on my bowed head. "Keep watch over her, Lord Jesus," he prayed under his breath and then as suddenly as I had felt the fear I found again my courage.

"That cry was woman to man, not child to priest. It is only honest to tell you so," I said, as I suddenly raised my head and threw another gauntlet that I knew would bring on another battle. "I hate myself for it."

"I wanted to win you for God and have you come to me then as a gift from Him, but it may have to be the other way round," was the answer he struck out at me with, and as he spoke he clasped my hand in his with a force that seemed to create the great silent, untenanted space around us as it had that night he had sung the Tristan music to me in the moonlight. "I'm going to save you and - and *have* you."

"No, no!" I cried, as I tried to draw my hand away, found it held beyond my effort and then suddenly released.

"I knew the first minute I looked into your eyes, but I'll wait," he said softly into the silence around us.

"No, no, don't even think such a thing," I exclaimed, and I wanted to rise to my feet and break the spell of that space around us, but I could only cower closer to him on the grass beneath the rustling silver leaves. "I'm going to marry Nickols in a few months and then I'm going out of this world of yours and you can lead them all to - to safety."

"No, it's in God's hands. He'll keep you and give you to me when the time comes. It all may mean suffering to us both, probably does, but I accept the cup - in His good time," and as he spoke he looked again into my eyes with a lonely sadness that I could not endure.

"I want to get away from you," I gasped and I felt that I must get out of the aloneness with him.

"We are in God's hands," he said again, as his warm hands found and held mine. "We must wait on Him with -" Then suddenly the world closed in on us again and we were on our feet - apart.

CHAPTER XIV

ABIDE WITH ME

"Auntie Charlotte, you stole Minister away from us in a no-fair way," stormed Charlotte as she came around the young larches and wild swamp root that had formed the world apart for the dangerous Jaguar and me. "Mother Spurlock can't sing to any good and Sue is so little we gets the key away from her. Let him come right back!" As she made this peremptory demand for the release of my prisoner, my name-daughter stood her ground with her cohorts, who had been scrambling around and over and through the shrubbery, massed behind her. There were Mikey of the red head, small James, the musical wee Susan, Maudie Burns and Jennie Todd, besides several more of the Burns family, a few Sprouls and Paynes and a very ragged young Jones, and they all looked at me with hostile and accusing eyes as Charlotte hurled a final invective at me. "You are wicked and the devil will burn you up," she threatened.

"He won't neither, at all. Hush up!" came a defense and a command in a very imperious young voice, and the Stray followed the voice from around the large trunk of the oldest graybeard. He had arrived late on the scene of action because his impedimenta had been the wriggling puppy of brindle hue, which he immediately released as he came over and stood between the Reverend Mr. Goodloe and me, with my hand in his own small paddie and defiance and defense to the limit in his high-held young head with its black crest and snapping violet eyes. At last I felt Charlotte had met her match and I

Maria Thompson Daviess

trembled for the result.

"She never stoled nothing," he further declared, looking Charlotte full in the eye.

"I meant she tooken him away, Stranger," parleyed Charlotte with extreme mildness for her and giving to the Stray the name that she had decided upon by translating the cognomen of his state into that of another almost equally forlorn. "My father told my Auntie Harriet that Aunt Charlotte would git Minister yet and I'll call the devil to stop her if she tries to get him away."

"I'll bust that devil's head with a rock and a bad smell," answered the Stray as he held tighter to my hand and hurled back his threat that held a remembrance of the conquering of the tenacious turtle.

"Auntie Harriet answered father that Auntie Charlotte and the devil could do most anything that -" small James was contributing to the general assault when with a wave of a calming hand Mr. Goodloe took the field.

"That will do, youngsters," he commanded with extreme mildness it seemed to me, considering the appalling situation. "I thought you had had about enough practice for to-day and Charlotte could have taught the little boy - er -"

"Stranger," prompted Charlotte.

"You could have taught him up to the point you knew so I could have a nice rest here under the lovely trees. Are you being kind to me in not helping me a little bit? You know what you promised me." And the beloved "Minister's" voice was just as grave and just as serious as if he had been reproving one of his deacons.

"Is talking to Auntie Charlotte and holding her hand the Lord's work?" demanded Charlotte, looking him straight in the face.

"Yes," answered Mr. Goodloe, gravely, looking her as straight in the eye as she had looked him.

"Then come on, Stranger, and learn the march without any tune but Sue," she said as she stretched out her hand to the Stray, who ignored it and clung to me with his serious eyes raised to mine.

"I'll go with you now over in the chapel and play for you on the organ and then we can all teach him," said the parson, and he picked wee Susan, the music box, up in his arms and buried his lips in the curls on the back of her fragrant little neck.

"Are you all done with Auntie Charlotte?" asked young Charlotte, with the extreme of consideration for him, not for my feelings.

"Yes, for the present," he answered, and he held out his free hand to the Stray, who was still clinging to me.

"Go with him, sonny, and Mikey will take you home," I said to my small champion, using the tender name that I had heard Martha give him. As I spoke I laid his hand in that of Mr. Goodloe and I didn't raise my eyes to his but turned from them and left him standing in the midst of his flock of lambs under the silver leaves and out in the bright light, while I went into the cool dark hall and on up to my own room which was also cool and dark.

"I am lost and blind and I don't know what to do," I murmured as I flung myself down on my window seat and looked through the narrow opening of the shutters out to the everlasting hills across the valley. "I know I am ineffective and perfectly worthless as I am but I will not, I will not be swayed by -"

"Charlotte," called father's voice with its commanding note

which had apparently come into it now to stay.

"Yes," I answered, and went down immediately, glad of the interruption to my self-communion and arraignment.

I found father and Nickols and Mark Morgan and Billy Harvey and Mr. Cockrell down in father's study and I could see from their faces that something unusual had happened.

"City Council voted the appropriation to meet Cockrell's and my donation for the schoolhouse, contracts have been signed and dirt is to be broken to-morrow by Henry Todd and thirty workmen Nickols has ordered down from the city," father announced, with jubilation in his voice. "We thought Goodloe was here in the garden with you."

"He was, but he has taken the children with him over to his chapel," I answered, and for some reason I blushed, for I saw Mark Morgan's eyes laughing at me and I also saw a glint I didn't like in Nickols' eyes.

"School to be opened on September twelfth and then let the kids fight it out," said Billy. "I bet on Charlotte to beat out the whole Settlement the first day if allowed full swing."

"If Goodloe didn't stand behind this mixing of - of social oil and - water, I'd be scared to death," said Mark.

"Mike Burns and Henry Todd and Spain had better be afraid of a loss of progeny," jeered Billy. "I bet Charlotte and James and the scions of the Sprouls and Paynes can lead the Settlement scions into by-paths of iniquity of which they never dreamed."

"I wish you had ten, blast you, for being so sensible as to have none," Mark answered him, and I felt rather than saw the bolt of pain that shot through Billy's heart. It's because Nell and her children are not his that Billy is bad, and what is going to help him?

"Well, let's go over to the parsonage and tell Goodloe all about it," father suggested, and the other men followed him out into the garden path that led through the Eden of my foremothers straight into that little Methodist chapel. Only Nickols remained with me upon the wide high vine-shadowed porch.

"I'll marry you the first of October, Nickols, and then we can go to France as you want to," I said to him without any preamble, and as I spoke I drew close to him as if for protection from something I didn't understand.

"Fleeing from the wrath to come?" questioned Nickols with a tender jeer as he took me in his arms and his lips sought the kiss I had been keeping from him. Again I refused it and he laughed as he pushed me from him and there was still more of the jeer in the laugh though the passion in his eyes was devouring and glad.

"Suppose we go north, right after Mr. Jeffries has finished his visit. Let's have the ideal village wedding. We'll have out the school children if any are left from the mix-up, and Goodloe can make us man and wife out here under the trees in our own garden. Then we'll go away from the whole show, the Christian religion included, and live happy ever after." And as he spoke Nickols again drew me to him and sought the kiss I still could not give him.

"Nickols, Mother Spurlock and poor little Mrs. Burns and - and Mr. Goodloe have something very real that we haven't," I faltered and, utterly weary, I laid my head down against his strong shoulder.

"That's what they say, but they can't prove it. They can't pass it on, so it mustn't really be anything. They are not tightwads, so they wouldn't hold back on us with their salvation, would they? Well, then, they haven't anything. It's all just a substitute for love, dear. Mother Spurlock fell back on it when she lost her husband. The little Burns woman wouldn't have it any more than Nell has if Mike Burns was like Mark Morgan. And

Goodloe would lose it in a week if - if he could get you in his arms." As Nickols spoke, his arms about me trembled and strained me to him.

"No!" I exclaimed as if I had heard blasphemy uttered.

"It *is*, dear, it is just suppressed sex. The scientists agree on that and all the religions are just that, from the most primitive to the most evolved. Some are more frank about it than others. The Igorrotes when they have their religious dancing at the mating season are more open than the Methodists about their being one and the same thing, but it all sums up alike. You can't get away from those facts."

"Then I want to be dead," I said as I drew myself from his arm and stood on the edge of the porch.

"Or you want to love," muttered Nickols under his breath as he watched me sullenly for a second. "Then it's October, is it?" he asked with one of his infectious, delicious laughs that have always broken across my serious moods and made them froth.

"Yes," I answered steadily.

"Then we'll tell Nell and Harriet and Jessie and Mrs. Sproul all about it, as I see them coming, on gossip bent I feel sure," he said as he went halfway down the walk to meet the girls before I could restrain him.

I shall always have with me the picture that Nickols made as he stood tall and handsome and smiling against the background of the wonderful garden he had helped to create, with the women smiling and clinging to him as he looked up at me with a great laughing light in his face. In some ways he was the handsomest man I had ever seen and his distinctions sat upon him as easily as the college honors of a boy. A wave of race pride and love swept up in my heart as I looked at him and I felt that in him must be the refuge that I sought. His sophistries always sank deep into me.

"Charlotte, my dear," said Mrs. Sproul, as I led her to a seat beneath the vines in a shady corner, "I wish I was sure that your mother knew of this safe happiness of yours. She adored Nickols and nothing could have given her a greater joy. And, my dear, for you to have held him against the world, as it were, is a triumph, I assure you. Always remember that men of his kind are - are desirable. I'll have a long talk with you before you go away with him." And I didn't know why, but the smile with which Mrs. Sproul whispered and patted my hand made me burn all over with protest.

"I wouldn't have you for a husband unless we were both convicted together to a chain gang for at least five years after the ceremony, Nickols Powers," said Harriet, with a laugh for which Nickols raised her hand to his lips as he responded.

"You like husbands in safety deposit vaults, don't you, Harriet?" At which sally they all laughed as they seated themselves around Mrs. Sproul and me.

"Why will women want husbands to be as stationary as - as hitching posts, Mrs. Sproul?" demanded Nickols as he leaned against one of the tall pillars and lighted a cigarette for himself after having lighted one for her and Jessie. Jessie Litton had always smoked, in secret until the last year or two, and Mrs. Sproul had frankly taken up the habit as a comfort for old age, she insisted. I suspect that she had had it for a long time in advance of the fashion. It was a really delicious sight to see the old world grace with which she accomplished it.

"Women have the nestling habit and that is why they want to believe men to be sturdy oaks in whose branches they can safely anchor a family as well as twine around in their affectionate gourd fashion," answered Mrs. Sproul, as she daintily puffed a smoke ring at Nickols.

"A lot of times the gourd vine grows so strong that she doesn't realize she is supporting her family by her own strength long after the oak has faded away in her coils and sprouted up from

Maria Thompson Daviess

an acorn in some other locality," said Jessie, as she, too, puffed a ring of smoke in Nickols' direction.

"Is this agriculture, biology or religion we are discussing?" demanded Harriet with a laugh as we all rose and went to the edge of the porch to meet Billy and Mark and father, who had with them the beloved "Minister."

"Congratulations and condolences, Mr. Powers," said Mrs. Sproul as she laid her hand in father's.

"On what score, my dear madam," he demanded.

"You know I asked for Charlotte on my fifteenth and her tenth birthday, Judge," Nickols said, with his ready grace in any situation, and he came and stood beside father and took his hand in his with the gentle affection a girl might have shown the older man. "You said 'yes' then and it has taken all these years to make her echo the word," and as he finished speaking he held out his arm and drew me close to father and himself.

"Hurrah!" exclaimed Mark, but I saw him exchange a glance of amusement with Harriet, and Nell gave him a warning little squeeze of the arm.

"Bless you both," said father, as he gave us both a hug.

All this I saw and noted before I raised my eyes to meet the jeweled eyes under dull gold that I knew were gazing straight at me as Gregory Goodloe stood in the background against the dark vine while the rejoicings over the announcement of my betrothal were enacted. Somehow I felt I could not make myself face their gaze, which yet I knew I must. I met a flash that burned down into the very darkest spots in my nature and illuminated them all. There was not a trace of male anger or demand in the gaze but a cold valuation of me and the entire situation that burned me as ice burns raw flesh, then over all of us there suddenly poured from the same source a tenderness that was as radiant as the summer sun.

"Yes, God bless us all!" he exclaimed, as he held out his hands to all of us, one of which Nickols took, with a swift challenging glance that in the radiance softened to confidence, and the other father took and fairly clung to in his happiness. I was glad, glad that I didn't have to endure the touch of his hand on mine after that glance, but not for one instant did my heart accuse his radiance of being dramatics. I rather felt that it came from a warmth within him by which everybody else in the world might be comforted but for which I would forever be cold.

"I *want* to be worth her, old man," Nickols said to him with a curiously pleading note in his voice, and he, too, seemed to me to be clinging to some of the strength that was not for me.

"Then God help you," was the answer given with the very essence of gentleness, but with a level glance into Nickols' eyes that was profoundly sad.

"And now let's hear the wedding plans," demanded Harriet. "This marrying and giving in marriage is the best way I know of to make time pass, and let's make Charlotte give us full measure. I'm matron of honor, of course, and I suggest only twelve bridesmaids. I intend to be preceded to the altar by Sue in an embroidered silk muslin I will provide, with a bonnet of tulle in which nestles a pink rose to match the ones in her basket. There will also be a display of pink knees that will be ravishing and -"

"Just let me remind you, Harriet, that this is Charlotte's wedding and not that of my daughter, Susan, and her often-mentioned knees," said Mark with a laugh that they all echoed.

"I am going to marry Susan's pink knees when they are ripe," remarked Billy and his suppression lasted long enough for me to attain command enough of myself to manage the plans of my own wedding.

Later when they had all gone by way of the chapel to help Mr.

Goodloe decide on some designs for a memorial window to his father he was having made by a great artist he and Nickols had selected, I went in to make my announcement to Mammy and Dabney.

"Well, ram in the cork to the demijohn, honey, and it'll be all right," was Dabney's semi-cordial consent, but Mammy went on industriously beating her biscuits for supper the one hundred and twenty licks prescribed by her reputation as a cook and her conscientious guarding of that same reputation.

"What do you say, Mammy?" I insisted on her giving her opinion.

"Of course, if you want to eat plain biscuits instead of the showbread from before the mercy seat - one hundred and two, one hundred and three -" was the answer given between the licks upon the white dough, and I fled before I should get a clearer manifestation of the disappointment I felt raging in her faithful old heart.

That night a young crescent moon was hung over the very crown of Old Harpeth as I threw the shutters of my window wide to the night breezes after I had put out my light and was ready for bed. I stood in its soft light and looked across to the dark mass of the chapel opposite and saw that a dim light was still burning from the window by the organ loft. And as I stood and looked, the empty place that I had felt in the very center of my heart grew colder and more bleak until suddenly across the garden on perfumed waves of sound came the Tristan love song and filled my emptiness with a pain that was both hot and cold. I stood and let the flood dash over me as long as I could and then with a sob I sank on the floor and rested my head on the window seat and began to weep as only women such as I know how to weep. Then into my sorrow very quietly there again stole another strain after the Tristan song had sobbed away into the night and suddenly my own weeping was stilled and again something within me was healed by the great tender voice singing out in the darkness beyond the hedge:

"Abide with me; fast falls the eventide -

Help of the helpless, O abide with me!"

"I don't know what to do, I don't know," I cried, and sobbed myself to sleep on my pillow after I had watched the light across the garden go out and after all in the little parsonage beyond the hedge was dark and quiet.

CHAPTER XV

A CLANDESTINE ADVENTURE

It seems a strange, almost savage thing that the few months before a woman's marriage are always filled so full of the doing of thousands and tens of thousands of small things that she has no time to think of the hugeness of the responsibilities she is assuming. Perhaps if she were given time to realize them she would never assume them. Once or twice in the long two, nearly three months that I had given myself to get ready to marry Nickols, I paused and found myself thinking of the weighty things of life, but I soon was able to shake off the thought of the future. The time I felt it press most heavily was one morning that Jessie Litton and I sat quietly sewing on some sort of fluff she and Harriet had planned for my adornment, and very suddenly Jessie laid down her ruffle and looked at me as she said:

"Charlotte, I would be frightened, positively frightened, at the prospect of marrying Nickols Powers."

"I am; but why would you be?" I asked her directly.

"I read that long resume of his work in the Review last night and for the first time I really realized what an important person he is to the development of American art. He really is a huge national machine and you'll be one of the important cogs on which the whole thing runs. You'll be ground and ground by his life and you'll have to make good or be responsible for some sort of a crash."

"No," I answered, slowly drawing my thread through the sheer cloth. "No, Nickols will live his own way regardless of the cogs on which it grinds. I shall have an enormous task in keeping up with the social side of his life, but Nickols is not the kind of a man who takes a woman into his work."

As I made my answer I was stabbed by the memory of the words that Gregory Goodloe had said to me on that day in the garden: "Separated from you, you going one way and I another, I can do nothing. You short-circuit my force - I am helpless without you." And *he* had been inviting me into the work for which he had been ordained into the holy Church of Christ. I felt myself groping blindly into the futility of my own life, and I was sick at heart.

"And if that is so, I would be still more frightened," Jessie said, gazing at me with dismayed and honest affection.

"Don't let's talk about it," I answered her and took up my sewing. At that moment and from that moment I cast myself into the whole whirl of activities in Goodloets and gave myself no more time or strength for self-communion. I was fleeing, and from what I dared not know.

And it was a busy month that stretched from August through September. Nickols said it would be his last fling at the old town and he proposed to leave his mark on its mossy sides. And he did.

In the first place money was pouring into little old Goodloets from three huge sources. The little one-horse tannery down by the river beyond the Settlement doubled, tripled and then quadrupled its capacity and next to it the little old saddle and harness factory in which Mr. Cockrell and old Mr. Sproul had been making saddles and harness since the days of the Confederacy, did the same and sent out consignment after consignment of saddles and bridles which were paid for in huge checks of Russian origin which almost paralyzed the Goodloets Bank and Trust Company and which worked pale Clive Harvey into the night until he managed to get young Henry Thornton in to assist him. His salary was raised three times until it was large enough to harbor Bessie and any number of small editions of them both, only she preferred to drink and dance and joy-ride with Hugh Payne, who could not have supported such a flowering by his own effort to have saved his own life and soul.

And then to burden poor Clive still further, Hampton Dibrell and Mr. Thornton hastily built huge pens over by the railroad and in these assembled hundreds and thousands of mules to be shipped through to France, which brought in return a steady stream of French francs to be translated into American dollars. Still further, Billy and Mark and Cliff, with Nickols' assistance, and the telegraph system, speculated in War Brides down on Wall Street until their individual bank accounts began to mount to giddy sums. Father and Mr. Sproul and more of the other men did likewise and Buford Cunningham got some spectacular returns from copper in Canada that Billy said would make Mrs. Buford Cunningham try to buy the Country Club outright for a summer home. And while there was prosperity in the Town the Settlement also had its share. Wages rose higher and higher and many of the women went to work at the machines in the saddle factory, leaving the care of the children to the old dames, which resulted in an added pandemonium in the Settlement streets.

"I don't know what is the matter. Goodloets is money mad," wailed Mother Spurlock, as she sank with weariness into the rocker on my porch one hot August afternoon. "The girls and the women are all at work and two babies have died this week from pure lack of mother's care, I might say mother's milk. Ed Jones' wife weaned her six-months'-old baby so she could go in the factory, and left it on condensed milk with old Mrs. Jones, who fed it incessantly and not at all cleanly. Now it is not expected to live. And they dance at the Last Chance until one o'clock almost every night. Is the world mad?"

"No, just prosperous, Mother Elsie," I answered her as I gave her a large fan and Dabney brought her a tall glass of very cold tea. "Little old Goodloets is having the same boom that the rest of America is getting from feeding and furnishing the rest of the warring world."

"Nickols Powers told me just last night that over two hundred thousand dollars would be spent on the improvements to this town in the next two months, counting the new schoolhouse, the restoration of the courthouse, the paving of the public square and the enlargement of the electric light plant. That doesn't count the money everybody is putting on their own private homes. That camp of workmen down by the river that Nickols has had sent down from the city has a hundred men in it now, and that is one thing that demoralizes the Settlement. Jacob Ensley has had that dance hall enlarged twice and he has employed George Spain to stand behind the bar. It is breaking Mrs. Spain's heart, but she is helpless, for George is being paid three dollars a day for being just where he wants to be. I don't know what to do. I firmly believe the town is mad, with only Gregory Goodloe to stand between it and God's wrath."

"What is he doing to stem the joy tide?" I asked with a laugh, for it did seem in a way funny to see one of the leading citizens of old Goodloets so distressed over its improvement and modernization through its enormous prosperity.

"He was down in the workmen's camp last night having a song service and seventy-five of them stayed there singing until midnight. Jacob had to put out his lights at eleven o'clock because there were not enough to pay to keep open. The chapel was full Sunday night and Jacob closed the Last Chance at six o'clock for the first time in its existence. The men passed it on to him to do it and he came and sat in a back pew himself. They all call Mr. Goodloe 'Parson,' and he walks in and around and about this town night and day shedding a kind of peace and good will even into the darkest corners. He lends a hand here and there with the work, eats out of the men's dinner pails when that Jefferson is too lazy to cook for him, or takes a bite off some stove down in the Settlement out of some old woman's pork and cabbage pot with just as much grace and heartiness as he eats at Nell Morgan's or Harriet Henderson's most elaborate dinners. And outside of his pulpit he never preaches; he just lives. This is what I heard Jacob say to him just yesterday:

"'Sure, and I wint up to set in one of your pews to see if your action in your own job was as good as it is in the many you lend a hand to week about.'

"'Well?' asked Mr. Goodloe, as he picked up, one of those rosy apples from the box Jacob keeps out on the sidewalk to blind the Last Chance.

"'I knows when to run and not be caught,' Jacob answered, as he put another apple in the parson's pocket and went back into the grocery door."

"Do you ever see Martha?" I asked with a kind of impatience. I had been three times down to the Last Chance and each time Jacob's excuses for Martha had been positive though courteous, and I had come away baffled, with the green groceries I had purchased as a blind to my visit. I had written to her and had had no response. At that I had stopped, with a self-sufficient feeling of a duty well done, but through it all I also felt that she was on the other side of a prison wall crying to me.

"Never," answered Mother Spurlock, with real pain in her voice. "She stays in that back room and cooks for Jacob, and the child stays with her and has only the small yard back of the bar in which to play. Jacob only let him come up to sing with Mr. Goodloe and the children a few times and now he is kept as near in prison as his mother. Jacob's attitude grows more morose about her and the child every day. I don't understand it. I never will. Martha was the loveliest girl that ever bloomed in the Settlement, and now she has been plucked and thrown into the dust. And the child is too young to share her prison fate. He must be got out and away."

"He will," I answered, with a calm confidence. I didn't tell Mother Spurlock, and I didn't know exactly why I didn't, but I was deeply involved in a clandestine affair with the Stray which was fast becoming one of the adventures of my life. It had begun in a positively weird manner and was continuing along the same lines. One morning several weeks after my first acquaintance and turtle adventure with him I had waked up at dawn and gone to look out of the window just as the morning star was fading over Old Harpeth. In the dim light I had spied a small figure down in the garden, hopping along by a row of early young rose bushes, with a can in one hand and a long stick in the other. Hastily getting into a few clothes I crept down through the silent house and out in the garden to find the Stray busily engaged in knocking large slugs off into a can.

"I feed 'em to mother's bird in the cage, 'cause he can't get out to get 'em," he explained. "They all sleep hard 'cause they work so late and I crawl out the window and go back while they don't wake up. I like your yard better than I do mine." The statement was made simply, without envy of apology.

And from that morning a queer kind of dawn life went on between the small boy and me. Morning after morning he threw a pebble to waken me and I hurried down to our tryst, which extended through the hour that lies between the crack of day and the first glint of the awakening sun. At first I had carried sweetmeats to our tryst, which were accepted with moderate pleasure, but one morning I had taken a huge volume of Rackham's Mother Goose which Nickols had brought me, and from then on our hour had been one of spiritual communion. I found the young mind insatiate and I had to ransack the library for stories and poems and pictures suitable to his years, though he rapidly developed a very advanced taste. The morning I read him the Shakespearian lines woven around the little Princes in the Tower, having suitably connected up the story for him with words of my own, we forgot the time and he overstayed his limit, for

Dabney was opening the house when he fled. For five mornings he did not come and I could find no way to get news of him. I asked Mikey and got a maddening response.

"They shut up Stray in the back yard because he's a shame to old Jake," was his answer to my question. "Jake would shoot anybody that climbed that fence."

"I bet I could get over and the bad man not see if I could get out in the dark," Charlotte declared as she stood listening to my questioning. "And I am going after Stranger that way, too, if ever they leave the front door to my house unlocked. It is wicked to shut up a little boy, and the devil would help me get him out." Charlotte's purpose was high if she did slightly mix her theology.

That night a wonderful thing happened in my moonlit room. I was dead asleep when I felt a soft hand stroking my face, and then my hair, and I awoke to find the Stray standing by my bed.

"They tied me in bed when they found out I had runned away in the mornings to see you, but I gnawed the rope that he put, because I wanted to tell you that I can go to the big school when it opens because Minister told him that he would be put in jail if I didn't. It is a law. I heard him last night, and mother cried a long time, for what, I don't know. Was she glad or sorry? Do you know?"

"No, darling, I don't know, and I wish I did," I answered him as I put my arms around him while he snuggled his black-crested head down beside mine on the pillow.

"My mother is sick, she cries so much," he said with a manly struggle that drowned the sob in his throat. "I don't know what to do. Do you know?"

"I'll find out," I said with a sudden fierceness as I strained him against my shoulder for an instant and then sat up in bed as if

I must do something at once.

"I must run right back and tie myself before he wakes up and whips me," the Stray said, and it sickened me to see him wrap the gnawed rope around his little arm.

"No!" I exclaimed, and held out my arms to him.

"I must, but I don't mind whippings if I can read books in school and you make mother not cry," and before I could stop him he ran out of the dim room and I could hear his cautious bare feet patter down the long stairway and hall.

That moonlight tryst was the last of the adventure, but I did not worry, for I knew that the school would be opened formally in ten days, and I had laid my plans for Stray in an interested friendship with the very competent young woman who had already come down from the state normal college to teach the amalgamated young ideas of Goodloets to shoot. Also, I had vague plans that hurt me, of getting Jessie or Harriet to continue the trysts for me after the wedding, whose details they were all pushing to completion by a mid-September day.

And added to the strenuosity of the laying of my plans for at least a year's absence, I had to help father make his arrange-ments for a six months' stay in Washington, for he had accepted the President's appointment on the Commerce Commission, and night and day he was at his library desk. The silver-topped decanter still stood on the sideboard in the dining room, and the silver ice bowl was formally filled before every meal by Dabney. The mint glass was kept fresh and fragrant but apparently father had forgotten entirely about all three. He ate twice as much as I had ever seen him consume and the worn lines in his face were slowly filling out into a delicious joviality. Mr. Hicks, the little tailor who had always clothed him, had little by little made over the outer man with new garments as the old ones grew restrictive, and Mother Spurlock had carried his entire discarded wardrobe, garment at a time, down to the Settlement for the clothing of some of her most needy friends.

But the most reborn person I had ever seen was Dabney. The little black man had lived so long under the shadow of father's moroseness that when the pressure was lifted from his bent black shoulders he rebounded to an amazing extent. His reaction took the form of gala attire in which Nickols encouraged him to the extent of silk hosiery of the most delicate shades from his own wardrobe, with ties to match, not to mention his own last year's Panama hat, pressed over into the extreme of the prevailing style for youthful masculine head adornment. Also Nickols bestowed upon him a very up-to-date Palm Beach suit, purchased at the Hicks shop, and on his first appearance in the kitchen for his wife's inspection I was present.

"Go take them clothes off, nigger, and put 'em along of my black silk shroud in the bottom drawer of the chist," she commanded, as she put her hands on her sixty-inch waist and stood before him with arms akimbo. "Folks is got no business to dress in life so fine that they shames they burying clothes."

"Shoo fly, I'm jest going to Washington, not to Heaven, in this here rig. When I git into Heaven it'll be 'cause I'm hiding behind that black silk skirt of your shroud, honey, if I'm as naked as borned," was the admiring, wily and also wholly sincere answer to Mammy's fling at the gorgeous raiment.

And while the Poplars teemed with wedding plans Nickols kept the whole village steamed up to be in readiness for the visit of Mr. Jeffries, which was dated for just a week before the wedding, and the village festival at the opening of the new school was to be the most important ceremonial of the whole visit. Father was to give him a dinner at which all of the Solons of the Harpeth Valley were to be present, and a ball at the Country Club was being planned by Billy with all enthusiasm. But the center of the buzz was down at Mother Spurlock's Little House, where Mr. Goodloe daily, and it seemed almost hourly, drilled the children for the ceremonial of the opening of their house of learning across the way from the Little House by the Road. Only echoes of the orgies reached the outside, and gossip ran high in the Settlement as well as the Town at the fragments that the delighted scions brought home, of curious folk dances mixed with fragments of weird tunes.

"Sure, a minister of the gospel to teach me Mikey to stand on one leg and spin around on the other with his hands over his head is a quare thing, but the Riverend Goodloe is no ordinary man," said Mrs. Burns to Mother Spurlock, who answered:

"You can trust him, Mrs. Burns, even with Mikey's legs."

And during all the long weeks of activity not once did I have a word alone with the Harpeth Jaguar. We met constantly at dinner at the tables of our friends and he came and went at the Poplars with the same freedom that Nickols enjoyed. He was long hours in the library with father, and somehow I felt that he was strengthening the structure that he had built on the ruined foundation and something passionate rose in my heart and filled it with pain every time I heard his ringing laugh come from the library table, accompanied by father's booming chuckle. Also, he worked early and late in the garden with Nickols and the young man from White Plains, and I saw that Nickols' artistic ideas flowed at top speed when Gregory Goodloe was standing by.

It was the same thing over at the new schoolhouse. Mr. Todd and the men worked miracles with their stone and mortar and wood and iron when he was standing by or lending a hand. The school was built partly of stone like the chapel and partly of old purple-pink brick like Mother Spurlock's Little House, and it was beamed with heavy timbers. It was roofed with heavy colonial clapboards which made it look as if it had already stood a century before the floors were laid or the very modern desks installed. It was built to house increasing generations, though only about fifty children would open its portals of education.

"It speaks of education de luxe, doesn't it?" Billy asked as Nell and Harriet and I stood with him and Nickols and the parson watching Mr. Todd directing the men in screwing down the desks just a few days before the opening.

"There is scarcely a village in England to compare with old Goodloets now, and nothing at all like it," said Nickols, as he looked first up the hill to the Town and down the hill to the Settlement. "I know that it is the first spot in America to express what the full grown nation is going to be. When we add beauty to the materially perfected mode of existence we are enjoying, life will be too short in the living. That schoolhouse ought to produce some results in art cultures in the infant mind of Goodloets."

"Yes, America is learning that the foundation of its national existence, trait upon trait, must be laid in the lives of the children," said Mr. Goodloe, slowly, and he smiled as across from the Little House came wee Susan's exquisite treble in a waltz song which was backed up by Mother Spurlock's bumble and Charlotte's none too accurate accompaniment. And we all smiled with him.

Always it seemed to me I was with him and a part of a number of people who felt the radiance of his loveliness, and not once had I for a second come into personal touch with him. I had, like the rest, got my smiles and friendliness from the dark eyes under dull gold, but the door to the land in which I had been with Tristan when he sang his death song had vanished and there were no traces of its portals. The only sign that was between him and me was his continued evasion of setting a date for the dedication of the chapel. He always answered inquiries by saying that the opening of the school must come first and when the dedication was mentioned he never looked in my direction. My soul seemed to be standing still and listening for something that never came.

And then Mr. Jeffries arrived on the scene of action.

That night of Billy's ball for the magnate, who was having the time of his gray-headed life under Billy's and Nickols' enthusiastic direction, the strange alien thing that had been developed in my depths, part unrest and part rebellion, since I had first looked into the eyes of the young Methodist parson, who had intruded himself and his chapel into my existence, got its death blow. In my presence Nickols made his formal request of the Reverend Mr. Goodloe to officiate at our marriage.

"Of course, Greg, old fellow, you are going to marry us next Tuesday, aren't you?" asked Nickols, as we stood on the steps of the Poplars after dinner, chatting with him as he was leaving to go over to the chapel while we went out to the dance. "I suppose there is some sort of formal way to make the request, but I don't know it."

"If there is I don't know it, either," was the kindly answer, which both Nickols and I took for assent.

"Thank you, sir," said Nickols, as he turned away towards father and Mr. Cockrell and Mr. Jeffries, who had come out on the porch with their cigars, and left him and me standing alone in the starlight.

"God guard you!" he said to me without taking the hand I held out to him in the darkness with a kind of desperation that seemed that of a drowning woman. "Good-bye!" and he was gone out into the night, leaving me, I knew, forever outside of his life.

"Wait, Oh wait!" I pleaded, but he was gone and I didn't even know if he heard the cry out into the velvet darkness.

That night was the most brilliant night that Goodloets had ever known. The Town was full of guests who had motored over from all the towns around in the Harpeth Valley. The Governor had come down from the capital in his huge touring car to congratulate father on his appointment and to meet Mr.

Jeffries. His adjutant-general and several of his aids were with him in their showy State Guard uniforms and all of the girls were rosy with excitement at the presence of so many rows of brass buttons. Mr. Jeffries opened the ball, and to the delight and amusement of us all, he succeeded in leading out with him Mrs. Sproul, who turned the opening dance into a stately old Virginia reel, which so delighted the tango dancers with its novelty that the dance was repeated several times during the evening by enthusiastic requests.

And while the Town reveled in celebration of the new Goodloets, down in the Settlement like rejoicings were being held at the dance hall of the Last Chance. In fact, the whole small city was in the throes of a great rejoicing. Why shouldn't all Goodloets revel when it was enjoying a prosperity beyond anybody's dreams of two years before? Everybody had been generous to the old town with the money that had come so easily from other suffering people's necessities, and security and good fellowship and prosperity reigned supreme. In each heart there was the feeling that now the old town and their personal lives were founded on solid rocks of peace and plenty and it was the time to eat, drink and be merry.

At supper the Governor's first toast, after that to the town itself, was to father and his distinctions. Then Mr. Jeffries toasted Nickols and me. He called Nickols the "American Wizard of Habitations," and, amid cheering and clapping hands, announced his intention to have Nickols build the American town on the Hudson. He called me the "Heart of the Achievement," and father's pride as he looked down the long table at Nickols and me was very wonderful and beautiful; and as great a pride rose in my heart as I saw him lift his glass of water to pledge me, leaving the bubbles breaking in his champagne.

It was very near dawn when we all motored home and it was upon the verge of the crack of day by the time Dabney and Nickols had got the Governor and Mr. Jeffries and the other guests settled under the wide roof of the Poplars, which had never hovered a more distinguished or brilliant house party.

For a few quiet minutes after they had all gone to their rooms Nickols and I stood alone on the front porch in the cool darkness with its hint of the dawn, while old Dabney shut up the back part of the house.

"The school festival will be over to-morrow, sweetheart, and the next day they will all be gone. The photographers are all through with the photographing and to-morrow night all the extra workmen go back to the city. There'll be three whole quiet days for you to get ready to give me that kiss, which I won't take when you are as tired as you are now," said Nickols, as he put a limp arm around me and leaned against the tall door post.

"To-morrow the old makes way for the new. Goodloets is dead! Long live Goodloets!" I answered, as I in turn leaned against Nickols' jaded arm for only a second before we preceded Dabney up the stairs to our rooms. In my room I went immediately to the window and opened wide the heavy shutters. I found myself looking down on Goodloets, which lay below the darkness of the Poplars like a long glowworm, brilliant with the lights from the homes of the revelers who were going to bed with a sense of perfect security. Still farther down the hill the lights from the Settlement glowed with scarcely less brilliancy and I felt sure that the Last Chance was still harboring a last fling of joy.

Suddenly over my spirit came a deep wave of depression that amounted to a great fear and then as I stood trembling in the darkness, a broad ray of morning light shot up over Paradise Ridge and spread rapidly into a crimson glow that was reflected against a black cloud hanging low over the head of Old Harpeth. A flash of lightning darted from the cloud and spread its gold fire through the crimson of the coming day, and then the sullen-pointed cloud sank rapidly below Paradise Ridge, over which it had risen, as if reconnoitering. Positively shuddering, I knelt against the window seat and watched the day come with a hitherto unknown terror. Then as I watched the dawn begin to drive away the sullen clouds a rich voice began to sing out beyond the old poplars as a window of the gray chapel was thrown open:

"Arise, my soul, arise,
Shake off thy guilty fears;

Before the throne my Surety stands
My name is written on His hands."

The calmness that came into my frightened heart was like the peace of a deep sleep, and with its strength I faced the day that was to be that of my humiliation and which was to be the crest of the wave of the high tide of Goodloets.

CHAPTER XVI

THE JEWEL IN THE MATRIX

When I awoke from a few hours of deep and exhausted sleep I found my room fast filling with the strenuosities of the day. In fact, I opened them upon Harriet Henderson, up, dressed and briskly doing. She had a large pasteboard box with her and the minute I brushed repose from my eyes she opened it and held up for my inspection a very short tulle garment besprinkled with tiny silk rosebuds, along with a bonnet and other wee but distinctly feminine paraphernalia to match. A basket adorned with a huge bow of tulle came from another box and I was forced to voice my admiration with the greatest vigor.

"How I'll ever keep from eating Sue up before she gets to the altar, I can't see," said Harriet, as she held the wee frock for a second against her breast. It hurts me to the quick of my own breast to see Harriet's eyes when she broods over Sue. I don't see how she is going to live life always as hungry as she is now.

"I suppose I might just as well wear my tennis things, because the guests will be already as completely enraptured as is humanly possible before my entry upon the scene of action of my own wedding," I said, as I sat up and took the small bonnet in my own hand. "It is too bad that Jessie and Letitia should worry themselves over my own wedding frock, if Susan is -" I was just saying when Nell arrived beside my bed with the Suckling in the very act of obtaining her early luncheon from the maternal fount. The nurse has always had to follow

Nell about with her successive hungry offspring.

"Girls, I really don't know what to do, but young Charlotte has given every single presentable garment that Jimmy possessed to different unclothed children in the Settlement, who were needed in the pageant, and Mark and Billy are laughing at her, while Jimmy is howling. I just ran in to see Harriet a minute and ask her if she -"

"Yes, Jimmie's wedding garments came home from Mrs. Burns' yesterday and I'll lend them to you just to spite those men, who are simply ruining Charlotte by the day," said Harriet, as Nell handed her the replete Suckling wrong end foremost and picked up the small tulle bonnet with a gurgle of maternal rapture that was in some ways as young as the happy gurgle that the Suckling gave as she settled into Harriet's dependable arms for her morning nap. Harriet cradled her against her own round, firm breast and for a second brooded then joined in Nell's rapture over the garments for the bedizening of wee Susan.

"If Harriet didn't dress and discipline my children I feel sure they would be found naked in a reform school," Nell said, with a happy and careless gratitude. There are some women to whom life is incidental and maternity the most casual adventure of all. The happy-go-lucky variety are apt to produce just such children as Charlotte or young James or Susan, and it is well if into their young lives there comes the hungry woman with a brooding mission.

"Young Charlotte will probably be the first woman governor of the state and -" Harriet was saying with a laugh when Letitia and Jessie arrived precipitately. Letitia had a parcel which contained a lingerie garment of mine, whose lace and embroidery and ribbon combined would have enraptured most women, and Jessie carried in her hand a package of belated wedding cards. They were followed closely by Mammy, who was in turn followed by the meek Sally. Mammy's address was delivered to me first.

"Git up quick, honey; the men folks has begun on the second round of waffles and they'll be calling for you. The day is on its shanks and a-going," she admonished, while Sallie turned on my bath.

"They are having breakfast out in the garden and the day is perfect. Do you want blue or pink ribbons in this Valenciennes set, Charlotte?" said Letitia, as she seated herself on the foot of my bed and drew out a ribbon bag whose contents were of many colors.

"A fashionable wedding is a white lie; you invite all the people you especially want to stay away," sighed Jessie, as she seated herself at my desk and lighted a cigarette, at which Mammy rolled her black eyes and departed with her nose in the air.

And while they all chatted over the sealing of my fate I arose and had my toilet made in my dressing room, in full hearing of the discussions about the best groupings of bridesmaids and the horror at the count of the cases of wine Billy had ordered from the city for the dinner to the groomsmen the night before the wedding.

"I adore Mark seven-tenths full, but I don't like to endure the end of the jag next morning," laughed Nell, as she began to put ribbons into the bodkins for Letitia. I saw Harriet give her a long look from under her half-lowered eyelashes as she hugged the Suckling closer to her breast. Billy had told Harriet and me casually a few nights before that "old Mark's drinking to a double-decker liver and a sidestep in his heart."

"Oh, gentlemen always drink in moderation. I never worry over Cliff," said Letitia complacently, as she tied a decorative shoulder knot.

"You expect to give him a daily dose of three drops on a lump of sugar, Letitia?" asked Harriet, as she exchanged glances with Jessie. One evening last week Jessie and Harriet had motored Cliff in from the Club just in time to save him from going over the riffles and Letitia had been dancing with him without noticing his staggers.

"There, that is the very last stitch to be taken on your trousseau, Charlotte," said Letitia, as she laid down the filmy garment she had been adorning with blue bowknots. "Press it, Sallie, and lay it with the rest of the set in the second tray of the medium-sized trunk. You can lock it and give me the key."

"I just can't stand it, Charlotte," said Jessie to me in a low voice, as I came from the hands of the skillful Sallie and stood beside the window next to the desk. "You are all I have got and only you - you understand. I can't give you up. I'm frightened."

"Hush - so am I," I answered her, as my hand gripped her shoulder under her heavy linen frock until I felt it must bruise it. Then I turned to the others, collected them and descended to finish breakfast with the Poplars' guests.

Never a more radiantly beautiful morning had spread its loveliness over the Harpeth Valley than the one I found out in the garden that twenty-seventh day of September, the gala day in the history of Goodloets. Huge white clouds drifted back and forth in a deep blue sky and they were rosy at times with the sunlight, but from some of the largest little tongues of lightning darted, while others were lit by what seemed to be an internal glow of fire. Cool winds, perfumed with the harvests and the ripening orchards and the vineyards out in the valley, rustled in the treetops and flaunted in the vines. The ardent sun seemed to be drawing from the bosom of the earth a hot mist which lay over the town like a filmy bridal veil, only stirred gently by the vagrant veering gusts of wind. Nature seemed to be holding herself in leash and only breathing upon the earth gently, as if to stir some latent lushness into autumnal activity.

"A perfect Harpeth day for Mr. Jeffries," said the Governor, as he came from his seat at the table to greet the girls and me.

The rest of the masculine breakfasters followed and I could see from the devastation of the table that they had all breakfasted well and to repletion. I also detected the worthless Jefferson, whom Mr. Goodloe had evidently loaned to his parents for the occasion, lift father's full glass of julep and drain it with one gulp, grab the half glass that Nickols had left, gulp it and begin on the finger or so in Billy's tumbler before Dabney could forcibly but quietly restrain him. In fact, I felt there would have been a riot among my servitors if Mr. Goodloe had not stepped aside and spoken a low word to Jefferson, which sent him busily at the table with his tray.

And from that moment Nickols' triumphant procession of inspection of Goodloets began. Mr. Jeffries stood in the middle of the reincarnated old garden, looked for a long time at the Poplars, which was like a green encrusted gem with its old purple red brick under the vines, glanced again and again at the chapel with its weathered stone that stood beyond the silver-leafed graybeards, then let his eye wander down the broad elm-bordered main street past the courthouse and past the Settlement to the river bending around it all.

"Money couldn't build anything like it, Powers," he said to Nickols at his side. "Time and gentle living have formed it as a jewel is made in a matrix. I was born in a mining camp, but I want you to start something like it all for my great grand-children to live in. How many generations will it take?"

"Give me five years, Mr. Jeffries," laughed Nickols in answer. "Greg Goodloe's great great grandfather and mine fought off the Indians from a stockade which stood where his chapel does now, but a year of modern life about represents a generation of pioneer endeavor."

"Not too fast, youngster, not too fast," said Mr. Jeffries, and I saw him exchange a grave glance with father. "What we Americans must have is stabilizers now that we have annihilated time. Without the discovery of something of that sort we will hurl along to destruction. What say you, Mr. Goodloe?"

"We have the same 'covert of wings' that David used when things spun too fast for him," answered Mr. Goodloe with the jeweled radiance that always came from his face when he spoke of his faith even casually. "Only 'where there is no vision the people perish,' and a people who invent flying machines and hold international law to account have vision. We don't know how much we've got, but it'll save us."

"After the material glass through which we see darkly is completely smashed for us," said father, with a curious sternness coming into his face that made me wonder. "But we must take Mr. Jeffries for a nearer inspection of our metropolis, be with Mrs. Sproul in time for luncheon and then help Mr. Goodloe open the institute of learning for young Goodloets."

In the motor cars parked before the tall gate of the Poplars all of the guests embarked for their review of the beauties of Goodloets. Nickols remained behind them while the half sober but skillful Jefferson wrestled with a slight tire trouble of his slim blue racer. For a few minutes we were alone in the center of the wonderful garden, which had never seemed so lovely as upon the day in which it had fulfilled its own and Nickols' destiny.

"To-day has brought just what I have longed for, have worked for and waited for, the commission for the spending of millions of dollars to make a little corner of the earth beautiful. Not a bad religion, that," said Nickols, as he told me that Jeffries had spoken a few words of decided business to him as he had packed him into Mr. Cockrell's car with father and Mr. Goodloe. "We'll take a honeymoon wander on the other side, as far from the machine guns as possible, and then I'll come home to begin my masterpiece." And as Nickols spoke his wonderful eyes glowed as he looked out at Paradise Ridge as if he were gazing into a radiant future - perhaps he saw a city not made with hands and did not - recognize it. "I see it all," he said, and put his arm around me while we started down the front walk as Jefferson pressed the horn to signal the readiness of the tire.

"I'm too busy to go with you, but I'll meet you at Mrs. Sproul's," a sudden impulse made me say, for I had intended until that instant to accompany him.

"A man can't eat his bride and have a trousseau, too," he laughed, as he drove off rapidly, leaving me standing by the old gate watching him. Then I turned and slowly walked out into the garden and down to the old graybeards. And seated on one of the grass mats I found the reason I had unconsciously been drawn back. Martha was waiting for me there.

"Why, Martha," I exclaimed, startled without understanding just why. "I might have gone and not known you were waiting. Why didn't you come and tell me you were here?"

"I couldn't - I found I couldn't," she answered me, looking up into my face with her strange, sad eyes. "I - I suppose I just came to peep in on you like I did to the coming-out party." She laughed softly, with a note of self-scorn in her voice.

"Is anything the matter with - with Sonny?" I asked quickly, again unconsciously using the name for the Stray that her tenderness had given him. Her white face and desperate manner frightened me.

"No, he's dressed in one of Jimmy Morgan's old suits and he is going to be taken from me this afternoon forever," she answered with the note of bitterness deepening.

"But you want him to go to school, don't you, Martha?" I asked patiently, as I sat down on a mat beside her. I spoke to her as one speaks to the limited intelligence of a child and I was slightly impatient at her distress.

"He asked me yesterday why everybody called him Stray and if it did mean Stranger like Charlotte said, and if he would always be called that or have an everyday name like Jimmy.

Soon he'll know and then I'll lose him as I'm losing everything else."

"Why won't you let me help you to - to begin over again?" I asked her, this time with less patience. "Why have you - you locked yourself away from me?"

"I can't - I won't ever tell you. I must go back, now I've seen you in - in your happiness. But I don't hate you - I never have." And as she spoke Martha rose and began to walk rapidly away from me.

"Oh, please don't go, Martha," I said. "In just three days I'll be going away for a long time, you know, and I want to help you in some way before I go. You ought to let me, and it worries me that you don't, now of all times," and as I put my selfish plea for ease to my conscience, something that was hot and rebellious made me want to stop the woman who was hurrying away from me.

"I won't, I won't make you unhappy - but I must go. I must! I'll - I'll be happy - and good now - if *you'll* only be happy. Good-bye!" And as she called back at me over her shoulder, Martha ran from me down through the hedge and into the door of the chapel, which always, night and day, rain and storm, stood slightly ajar. A queer pain smote me to see that she had run from me into the only place in all the broad, smiling Harpeth Valley where I could not - or would not, follow her. And the sanctuary that she sought was for every man, woman or child who wanted it - only I could not and would not seek it.

"'The covert of wings,'" I whispered to myself, as I went down the street to Mrs. Sproul's as rapidly as possible to be rid of my own company. As I repeated the words that the parson had used to Mr. Jeffries I noticed one great white cloud with a dark center flash fire into another, to a great crashing and rumbling. "I wonder if it is really going to storm," I speculated gloomily, as I turned into the Sproul gate, but the brilliant sunshine seemed to fling me a dazzling denial from every petal of the white clematis that wreathed itself across the front porch, under which Mrs. Sproul, arrayed in all the midday magnificence of good form, sat and waited for her guests. Mrs. Cockrell sat beside her and they were delighted to see me and demanded happiness from me which it was hard for me to give from the depths that had been stirred by my strange interview with Martha, to which I felt I ought to have a key, but could not find it anywhere.

CHAPTER XVII

THE PAGEANT

"We were just saying, Charlotte dear, that this absurd school affair has completely overshadowed your wedding day," said Mrs. Cockrell, as she rocked back and forth in tune with her Irish point rose she was constructing. "It seems to me a wedding ought to come before a school festivity."

"Social law requires that marriage take precedence of schooling," said Mrs. Sproul, as her mischievous old eyes snapped at Mrs. Cockrell's placid conventionality. "The correct order is for women to take husbands and then school children should be the inevitable outcome. They are not, however, in this day and generation, which is about to be the last, I'm thinking."

"There will be thirty-nine kiddies from the Settlement and eleven from the Town to feast on reason and flow soul together in the new school," I laughed, as I sat down between them. "Also I'm thinking that a lot more will be forthcoming from the Settlement by next week. Young Charlotte and Mother Spurlock clothed as far as they could, but they will keep at it, I feel sure. I feel guilty at the idea of taking three trunks of clothes away from the watchful eye of Mother Elsie, only I'm leaving the accumulation of years for her distribution."

"The passport to Elsie Spurlock's heart is a condition

composed of rags, hunger and unhappiness. She has no sympathy or time for a sanitary and contented friend," said Mrs. Sproul with a decided tartness that was only a reflex of the deep affection she bore the mistress of the Little House, which had existed since childhood and would endure.

"I hear some of the cars coming," announced Mrs. Cockrell, as she began to crochet furiously at the last petal of a rose. "Is my cap straight? I do so want to finish this row and can't go in to look."

"You'll put out St. Peter's eye with a crochet needle while he's unlocking the pearly gates for you, Lettie Cockrell," said Mrs. Sproul, as she rose and stood with ceremony at the head of the steps to meet the Governor and Mr. Jeffries and father as they came up her front walk.

Mrs. Sproul always has the most delightful old world sort of midday dinners and it was two o'clock before we all arose from her long table, at one end of which had been demolished a spiced ham and from the other end had disappeared two fat summer turkeys. A saddle of lamb had been passed in between and we had wound up with sweet potato custards, apple float and ice cream.

"I understand now," said Mr. Jeffries, as his keen old eyes twinkled down the table at Nickols. "This food should produce geniuses. The South feeds for it."

"Yes, we eat, drink, are merry and do it all over again to-morrow," said Mark, as he walked beside Mrs. Sproul from the devastated dining room. "And we must all hurry if we are to see your young ideas begin to shoot. This day isn't really hot, but just thinks it is. Look at those clouds boiling up back of Old Harpeth as if wanting to storm, but afraid to begin it. There's not a breath of air stirring. Wish it *would* shower, for I believe the colors of Goodloe's pageant would run and I'd like to see the true hue of this melee of his come out in the wash. It would do Charlotte good to fade a bit. She has been hectic

Maria Thompson Daviess

since daylight and the rest of my juvenile family with her. Jimmy is S and Z in the alphabet and Sue has got a huge A sewed on her back. Goodloe intends that education shall be nailed to 'em."

And at his admonition to hurry and the alluring description of the entertainment to come, we all betook ourselves on foot toward the schoolhouse down the street a few blocks, halfway between the Town and the Settlement.

And as we went all the rest of the Town hurried out of wide, high, vine-covered doors, down broad, flower-lined walks, and joined us from under bowers of blooming roses, honeysuckle and clematis. We actually approached the schoolhouse in the form of quite a large procession, and as we wound our way down the hill we met a like procession winding itself up the hill from the Settlement, a procession arrayed in its best bib, tucker and boiled shirt, just as we were adorned in silk, lace, fine muslin and linen.

"It looks like two armies approaching each other - Greek is going to meet Greek," said Billy.

"Rather Greek meets Vandal, and there stands Goodloe to do the interpreting," Nickols jeered in answer.

And as we all flocked into the wide gate of the school yard I was again struck with the great beauty of the tall, broad, lithe, free man who stood in the middle of the walk just inside, welcoming Town and Settlement alike. And while he greeted us, his enthusiastic flock of older children seated the groups of guests on the long rough benches which were placed facing the door of the schoolhouse, leaving a wide space at the foot of the steps, which was roped off with golden chains of black-eyed daisies and which was evidently to be used as a stage for the pageant.

"Just look how Goodloe is failing to mix his oil and water," Nickols whispered to me, as we observed all of the Settlement groups gravely gravitate to the left side of the walk while all the Town in chattering parties took seats on the right. "That's right, Burns, take off my last summer coat," he added, still in a whisper to me as the Burns parent struggled out of the unendurable gift garment and thus gave a signal that whipped off every coat on the left side of the walk in the twinkling of an eye, to the evident distress of the tightly girted and uncomfortable but more formal feminine members of the Settlement contingent. Conjugal strife was about to make its appearance when Mother Spurlock, who was seated beside poor little Hettie Garrett, holding the Mother Only in her arms with never a glance for Mrs. Sproul, who had beckoned her to a seat next to her own beruffled silk skirts, passed the word around that such comfort was to be accorded the masculine guests. Even with such sanction, however, Luella May Spain looked pained at her father's gay new red suspenders, and I could see that Mr. Todd's striped shirt was hurting the feelings of Sadie Todd dreadfully, and she and Luella May returned Billy's gallant salute with the greatest embarrassment. And in all the buzz I found myself looking anxiously for Martha Ensley's pale face and dark eyes, but failed to find them.

"This is one place she ought not to have to peep into; here she has the rights of her citizenship and her motherhood," I said to myself.

But if the Town and the Settlement sat in the seats of the audience, divided by the walk as were the walls of waters by the dry path along which Moses led his chosen people out of the darkness of Egypt, such a division was not noticeable among the performers of the pageant who were supposed to be in hiding with their costumes behind a tall screen of shrubs at one side of the schoolhouse, but who bubbled out on all sides. Charlotte appeared once holding small Maudie Burns in a comforting embrace and guided her to her mother for some sort of attention to the very short skirts of blue gingham which were draped with about ten yards of green crepe paper, while both Harriet and I gasped as we saw Mikey jauntily hand the Suckling, tightly wrapped in brown swaddlings, into the rapturous and tender embrace of Katie Moore, who had blue wings sewed to her small gingham shoulders.

"Great Guns! They've got Sucks in it, too!" gasped Billy. "That child is too young to educate and Goodloe ought to be restrained from cradle-snatching like -"

But just here Billy was interrupted and the audience all quieted down as Mr. Goodloe, in his white flannels and with his gold head ablaze in the sun, which suddenly shone out fiercely from behind a white cloud which was sheeting internally with electricity, mounted two of the front steps of the schoolhouse and held up his hand for silence.

"Mr. Todd," he said with beautiful deference, "will you lead us in prayer?" There was a perceptible rustle of feeling on the Settlement side of the walk, for Mr. Todd was one of the parson's deacons, but he had also been the master workman in the building of the schoolhouse, and his neighbors were quick to respond to the tribute offered him before the distinguished men present. He rose, gaunt and grizzled in his shirt sleeves, but what he said was brief and as square-cut and to the point as any nail he had ever driven. I saw the Governor and father exchange glances and I noticed when the Governor responded to his call he was much less ornate of speech than usual and much more universal. They all spoke, from Nickols along the line to father, and after repeated urgings Mother Spurlock rose to the occasion, and by way of making the Town and Settlement at home in its new joint quarters announced that the tea canister with its slit would hereafter be nailed just inside the schoolhouse door.

The laugh and delighted applause that was given her seemed to have been the last straw to the actors behind the shrubbery, restrained by their young preceptress, for the pageant broke upon us.

First Mikey, with huge white cambric stork wings, hopped upon the stage of sward and deposited the brown-wrapped

Suckling in a hollow log in the center, and departed flapping. After that the ceremonial developed itself into the education that was to flow down upon her defenseless head at the waving of the wand of Minerva, who was Charlotte with a tinsel star of wisdom resting rampantly upon her brow. And it came down upon the Suckling with a vengeance. A whole troop of young letters of the alphabet, led by small Susan with the large red A upon her fat back, danced around the Suckling's helplessness and finally backed up to the audience to spell the word "Reading." Next in hopped a flock of numerals led by the indefatigable Mikey, which backed up and presented themselves from one to ten to thus imply the hated science of "Arithmetic."

The Suckling slept on amid delighted gurgles from her mother and Harriet. She slept through a presentation of the script letters of "Writing" and was still unconscious when "Geography" in crepe paper, with flags of all nations, grouped around her. She only awoke when, all by himself, sturdily, with his head in the air and fairly radiant with beauty and courage, the Stray marched upon the scene, rolled into a white roll of paper and girt about with a broad red ribbon sealed upon his back to represent "Diploma." Silently and intent upon his duty he walked straight to the Suckling in her log crib, bent over her, crooned to her reassuringly a second, lifted her in his white arms and backed off behind a tall laurel bush with her nodding in delight over his shoulder. The boy was so beautiful and the little scene so tender that the entire audience caught its breath at its - audacity. A gauntlet had been thrown into the faces of both the Town and Settlement and they both understood.

They sat perfectly still with astonishment while the performers were being massed in the schoolhouse by the young teacher for their final march out to the steps for the hymn singing with the beloved "Minister," which was to conclude the ceremonials.

And while the audience sat awaiting the further presentations

Maria Thompson Daviess

to be made them by their offspring, Mr. Goodloe came out the door and halfway down the steps. Then suddenly he stopped and looked out over the valley with such an expression on his face that with one accord his audience rose and looked with him. And as it looked a groan came that was a chorus melted into one voice of terror, while all of them stood helpless with amazement. While we had all been sitting in the curious sweltering heat, watching with pride a future for our children being foretold for them by themselves, death had reared itself behind Old Harpeth, coiled itself into a huge black spiral of thunder and lightning and was driving down the valley upon Goodloets with a velocity that defied the eyes to follow. For a long second every man and woman stood rooted to his foothold on the earth and watched the tornado strike the edge of the Settlement, smash down the saddlery as if it were a house of cards, and churn the little tannery into the river. Then as it grasped the roof of the Last Chance and began twisting it with a roar that grew in volume every instant, Gregory Goodloe suddenly raised his hand and spoke in a perfectly calm voice that rang out above the groan of the tortured shanties of the Settlement which were crashing down against each other.

"Oh, God, we trust in the covert of thy wings," he prayed for a second and then commanded: "Fall to the earth, all of you, and let it pass over you!"

"The children!" came a cry that was a wail of parenthood, as we all sank to the ground just as the terrible black monster tore the roof from the Little House and hurled it toward us across the street. I saw a huge rafter hurtle through the air and strike down Mark Morgan as he started toward the steps of the schoolhouse, and by not a half inch did it miss drunken, useless Mike Burns as it fell beside him. Then I covered my eyes as the cloud and the wind passed over me and I only heard it strike and rend and crash and tear the schoolhouse, beam from beam and stone from stone. An eerie wail of the voices of little children was mixed with the roar of the monster which crashed on up through the Town, laying low the homes of our pride and prosperity, leaving us with our faces to the ground while upon us began to pour a deluge of cold rain.

"Mark! Mark!" I heard Harriet moan beside me and I saw her crawl under the wind toward where Mark had fallen.

"My babies, Oh, my babies!" came a wail in Nell's voice, and I saw her try to rise, be knocked over by the wind and then begin to crawl toward the wrecked mass that a second before had been the schoolhouse and from which now could be heard the screams and cries of the children. Then as suddenly as it had laid us low the cruel wind left us and with one accord we all sprang to our feet and surged toward the children's calls and cries that came out to us in the semi-darkness that still enveloped us, though both the wind and the rain were abating.

But before a huge slab that had been the top step of the schoolhouse we were all halted by a voice so stern and commanding that even the agonized mothers and fathers paused.

"Stop! Not a man or a woman must come a step nearer," said the parson, with the authority in his voice that must always be obeyed when used by one human being to another. "The roof of the house has split and sunk in the middle and only one side beam is supporting it. If it is touched by so much as a hand it may lose its balance and fall on the children. Only one man must come forward and put his shoulder under the beam at the other end while I hold this. The children must come out one by one, so as not to shake anything on them. The beam may fall. Do you all understand me? One man!"

"Me, Parson, me!" demanded Mr. Todd.

"A broader, younger man, Todd," answered the parson, and he was casting his eye over the huddled people before him when a wail came clear and distinct from within the ruin.

"Stranger is caught and bleeding! Hurry, hurry!" were the

words that Charlotte sent forth with all the strength of her young lungs.

"It's my child, Oh, it's mine!" came an answering, cry, and from behind some hiding place Martha Ensley flung herself across the front of the huddled group of the Settlement people and against the defense of Gregory Goodloe's strong arm which held her from the tottering doorway he was supporting. "Let me get him out!"

"No, Martha," the parson said calmly and tenderly, as he held her back.

"Then *you* come and get him," Martha said, as she suddenly straightened herself and looked out among us of the Town. "He's yours - come and save him!" But even in her agony she was cautious in her appeal, which came without the demand of a name. We all held our breath for an instant, Settlement and Town. Who would answer her?

CHAPTER XVIII

LIGHT - INTO DARKNESS

"Yes, Martha," came the answer after an instant's pause, and Nickols Powers stepped from my side to that of Martha Ensley and took her wrung hands in his. For another long moment we all stood tense at the acknowledgment that the tragedy had forced to the surface. I stood beside father like a woman of ice, yet on fire with a contemptuous humiliation. The eyes of all my world were for an instant turned on me, then they were all called back to the tragedy that was tottering over us.

"Hurry, hurry!" came another wail from within the ruins in Charlotte's voice. "He's bleeding!"

Again Martha started to fling herself past Nickols and the parson with a scream of terror which was faintly echoed from within.

"Somebody come to Martha," commanded Mr. Goodloe, as he held her off with one hand while he eased the beam on his shoulder so that Nickols could slip in past him to the other end.

Suddenly a great, beautiful warmth melted the horror of pride and humiliation that had frozen my heart as Nickols had stepped from my side to that of Martha in acknowledgment of her claim upon him for the saving of the child. All fear for her or us or the babies passed from me. My soul had gone out into a darkness, called on some great Power that must be there directing such a thing as was happening to us, and calm and clear the answer of courage flowed into me.

Then without another moment's hesitation I stepped forward and held out my arms to Gregory Goodloe for Martha. He put her into their strong embrace and I pressed her head down upon my shoulder in a great tenderness I had never felt before, while Nickols, with a long, hunted look at us both, crawled into the crumbling ruin and crouched under the beam as Gregory Goodloe directed him.

The wind had died down, the clouds were rolling away the darkness and the rain had almost stopped as we all stood and waited for Gregory Goodloe to bring from that ruin, in the way his superior judgment thought best, either life or death. From within there came sobs and smothered little moans that were so mingled that they could not be identified by even the mother hearts held at bay by the faith that made them obey the parson's command.

And then as I stood there with the mother of the child of my lover cowering against my breast, with the man who in a few days was to have been my husband, crouched under almost certain grinding death, and looked into what at any moment might be the grave of all the babies of the women I held dear, a light was flooding into my darkness and all of the obscure, untranslatable writings on my nature became clear and I received my consciousness of my Master, the Lord Jesus, with a cry that I sent up for His mediation for the lives of the little ones. It was my first prayer.

"O Christ in Heaven, help save them!" I pleaded. "Quick, Gregory, quick!" I added another supplication in the next breath.

"Sue is bleeding, too!" again came a wail in Charlotte's voice. "Mikey's got the baby, but he's caught."

Nell had been kneeling beside Mark's prostrate form, but at Charlotte's call she laid his head on Harriet's breast and flung herself against my arm outstretched to receive and restrain her.

"Now, Nickols, steady! I'll lift them past the beam," said the parson, as he braced himself in the door space which had been crushed into a narrow opening.

"Charlotte, take the baby from Mikey and hand her to me first," he commanded. "Where are you caught, Mikey?"

"Me leg," wailed Mikey and his wail was echoed by poor little Mrs. Burns.

"Here," said the parson, as he handed the brown swaddled bundle to Nell, who caught it in her arms and sank shuddering to my feet.

"Now, Charlotte, I want you to get all the other children who are not caught into line and make them walk carefully, just as you did here to me," said the parson in a perfectly calm voice, the one he had used to command his small congregation in the weeks of the drill.

"They are all crying and got their heads covered up," answered Charlotte in despair. "They won't get up and march." Loud wails of fear and anguish accompanied this statement, as if to corroborate it.

"Sing with me, Susan, sing the march," came the command without an instant's delay from the lips of the beloved Minister.

> "Onward, Christian soldiers
> Marching as to war,
> With the cross of Jesus
> Going on before -"

came wee Sue's high, sweet voice which rose from the cavern

and joined with the parson's in the old song that has led strong men through many a death watch.

For a long moment we all waited and then out of the hole in the mass of stones and timbers and bricks, led by wee bleeding Susan, crawled a slow stream of bloody, bruised, sobbing infant humanity to be absorbed with cries of rapture into waiting arms.

"Hurry, Goodloe, get the boy and Charlotte; my God, hurry, the beam is sinking!" came in Nickols' smothered voice.

Martha started, but I held her tight against my breast.

"I've got Mikey's pants loose with my teeth," came in Charlotte's voice, as a creaking of the timbers made a shudder run through the waiting crowd as every man and woman who held a restored treasure close, waited to see what would happen to the three left in the settling ruins.

"Come out, Mikey, come out," called the Burns paternal parent.

"I won't! I'm going to help Charlotte git out Stray," was the undutiful response of courage to the craven.

"Where is he caught, Charlotte?" asked the parson, as he edged a little farther under the beam, which tottered and brought him to a cautious standstill.

"His middle. Mikey's pushing and I'm pulling, but he's all bluggy. He's dead all but his toes that wiggle."

"Hurry, Goodloe, hurry!" groaned Nickols, with what seemed a final inspiration of breath.

"Pull him loose and come quick, Charlotte, you and Mikey. Never mind the blood," was the firm command and in a few seconds Charlotte and Mikey squeezed through the fast closing opening, bloody and torn, but with the limp Stray dragged between them. A great cheer went up as Martha turned and caught the unconscious boy in her arms, then it froze in the throats that had been uttering it. Slowly, but more rapidly than could be stayed by human hands, the whole heavy roof crushed down upon the rest of the ruin; and under it and the beam went Nickols Powers with only one deep groan. Mr. Goodloe tried to hold up the whole side of the roof on his own shoulders and only staggered out from the very brink of being involved in the crash. Martha sank to the ground and hid her head in my knees and sobbed while I heard a great cry break from my father's lips. Nickols was the last of his race and our pride was blasted when he fell.

"Now forward, every man of you, but lift and dig carefully," commanded the parson, as he stood on the very edge of the ruin. "Todd, you stand at the corner and show them how to roll back the timbers to the right. Carefully, men, but quick, quick, and with the help of God!"

It seemed hours that the men wrestled with the timbers and tore away brick and stone and steel, but it was only a few minutes before they pried up a section of the heavy roof and lifted Nickols from the debris beneath.

"He's breathing," said Mr. Todd, as he laid him in the parson's great, strong, outstretched arms open to receive him and which bore him out through the crowd swiftly and laid him across the seats of Nickols' car. Doctor Harding had just put Mark, a limp, heavy body, into his own car, with Harriet to support the bleeding head, and Nell crouched beside him with the Suckling in her arms, and sent them on up into the devastated Town. Now he came and helped us settle Nickols on his cushions.

"Shall I send my car and Colonel Leftwick for surgeons and nurses from the Capital?" asked the Governor. "How is it with Morgan?"

Maria Thompson Daviess

"He is dead," answered the old doctor with the calm serenity that he had acquired after so many years of giving up his friends. "This case is another matter. There may be a chance and I'll need help. We don't yet know how many more are injured in the whole town. We'll need help."

"Then I'll drive for it myself," answered the Governor, as he swung into his powerful car and started it out into the valley. "I'll make it back in six hours. No other man can drive this car as fast as I can."

And true to his promise, he was back within the time with nurses and surgeons and supplies of all kinds. By that time the whole Harpeth Valley had heard of our tragedy and all who could find a way were hurrying to our rescue or comforting.

The dawn of the beautiful new day found Nickols still alive, stretched on his bed in his own wing of the Poplars, which alone of all the homes in the Town had not been touched by the storm monster. The old house stood unharmed in all its beauty in its garden which had hardly a leaf or a branch broken, and hovered under its roof the last of the name of its builders. He lay quiet and unconscious while his life jetted itself away from a great hole in his lung made by a splinter from the beam he had held up until old Goodloet's children had been given back to its future. The great surgeon who had come down with the Governor, watched, shook his head and went at his task again and again with a dogged courage. For an hour he would leave him to go and help Dr. Harding with some of the other injured, but back he would come to his fight for Nickols' life.

And all over the stricken town there were similar tragedies being enacted. Over at the Morgans Mark lay cold and still in the long parlor, which was almost the only part of the handsome old house left intact by the tornado, and Harriet sat beside him while Nell nursed maimed wee Susan and torn Jimmy, and restrained Charlotte from injuring her sorely twisted ankle.

Down at the Last Chance, Jacob Ensley was stretched upon a bed in the bar with a sheet drawn straight and decorously over his bruised white head. He had been killed by a blow from a roof timber, while from right beside him young George Spain had been rescued unharmed. When he had crawled from the ruins he had held in his hand a bottle of whiskey which he had just uncorked for his own and Jacob's refreshment when the tornado tore at the East Chance, and scarcely a drop had been spilt. And the tornado had displayed the vagaries of its kind.

Old Granny Todd had been lifted in her rocking chair and carried halfway over the Town and left beside the Spain cottage with her feeble life intact, while Mrs. Spain, upon whose shoulders the burden of mothering all seven of the Spains rested heavily, had had one of those valuable shoulders broken and was left crushed and bleeding beside the rocking chair in which the helpless old dame arrived for her enforced visit. The household goods of one family had been torn from them and thrown into the melee of another, and the Jamison clock was found ticking busily away over on the roof of the Todd's chicken house. A girl mother in a little cottage on the edge of the river bank was found floating against the shore in her wooden bedstead, drowned, while near her the little two days' old life had been perfectly preserved upon the pillow in the rocking chair where it had been sleeping when the great storm beast had made its raid.

And all Goodloets mourned, crying for her children, and would not be comforted. The second day after the storm the dead were buried. Mr. Goodloe, with old Mr. Stokes, the Presbyterian minister, on one hand, and the Baptist student preacher on the other, stood in the center of the beautiful city of the dead, over which the storm had passed unheeding, and had services for the rich and the poor alike. With the same ceremonial were buried Mark Morgan and Jacob Ensley, and the girl mother, Ted Montgomery, who had been struck down by the falling sign of the Bank and Trust Company on Main Street, and a score of others.

Then after all the tears had been shed and the sobs had ceased, all the flowers strewn and the reluctant feet had left the silent city, I went over behind the tall cedars into a corner and knelt beside Martha Ensley, who had flung herself down across the new-made grave that held all that was left of Jacob Ensley, the man who had bulwarked sin in his Settlement and menaced all of Goodloets for many a year. The wide-eyed boy crouched beside her and I took his hand in mine.

"Martha," I said, as I bent beside her in the twilight. "I want you to come home with me, you and Sonny. Your place is there now and you must bring him." All day I had thought and I had prayed to be aided in doing what I knew was best.

"Oh, no, Miss Charlotte, no," she said, and shrank from my arms.

"Yes, Martha," I said, and drew her closer.

"It happened the summer we were all first grown and you were in Europe. I couldn't fight him off. I knew he belonged to you and I loved you, but I couldn't fight him off," she sobbed and the Stray's little arms went around her neck.

"I'll fight fer you - I'll fight," he said, with brave, wonderment in his eyes and voice.

"I went away this summer and I wanted to stay. Mr. Goodloe tried to help me, but Nickols found where I was and made me come back. It was wrong to you and I knew it. I stayed shut up in my room, but he would come. And I sent him to his death. He was yours and I killed him for you! Please go away and leave me!" And again Martha cowered away from me.

"Nobody need know you are in the house, Martha, but you must come with me," I said, and I spoke with such quiet authority that she rose and followed me out of the shadows into the starlit night which had come down over stricken Goodloets. I found Billy waiting for me in his car and he spoke gently to Martha and settled her and the boy on the back seat with never a question in his kind eyes.

"God, you women!" he said to me under his breath, but I avoided his eye and he drove us silently to the Poplars. The long halls were quiet and empty in the anxious hush of the whole house which was keeping its life - or death watch. I led Martha to the room that opened into mine, in which all of the girl guests of the Poplars always slept, and made her take off her hat and make the boy comfortable. Then I went for Dabney and asked him to take food to them.

"Yes'm, I will. God love my little miss," was his answer, and I knew that I could trust his kindness to Martha and the boy.

Then I went into the library to father. I found Mr. Goodloe with him and father's calm under his anxious suffering gave me a thrill at the thought of the regained strength it implied. The parson's face was grave, but full of a white light from the fire burning back under the dull gold brows. His warm hands took my cold ones in them and pressed them palm to palm in the attitude of prayer and very tenderly, from his soul to mine, he said:

"'The Lord is good, for his mercy endureth forever.'"

"Forever?" I asked him, looking up with the child's faith that had been born in my heart shining in the confidence in my eyes.

"Forever," he answered me with quiet authority.

"Yes," said father solemnly, as if himself reassured after doubts. Then, after a second's pause: "Daughter, Nickols is conscious and is asking for you. Will you go to him?"

I took my hands out of those which had given to mine the strength of prayer and went.

CHAPTER XIX

THE SPARK AND THE BLAZE

I found Nickols lying in his own dim and high bedroom, perfectly motionless under the white sheet, as he had been for two days, the only difference that now his great dark eyes burned into mine and on his mouth there rested a faint trace of the old mocking smile. I sat down close beside his pillow on a low chair which the nurse placed for me as she gave me a warning look and left us alone.

"This is your wedding day, Charlotte, and the license is over on the desk to destroy," he said, with the mocking light in his eyes flaring up into greater strength. "I suppose you are duly grateful for the merciful escape accorded you."

"Please don't, dear," I said, and I reached out and took his burning hand in mine.

"You never really cared, Charlotte. You cold women make havoc in a man's life. I've no excuses to make, but I wish I could hear you say that you forgive me. I'd go out more contentedly." And the light that sprang up into his face showed me just what a hold I had on his loyalty and the thing a man calls his honor. And it came to me on the wings of a quick, silent prayer, prayed in a heart unlearned in the forms of petitions, that I must make a fight to give him the peace of his heritage of immortality before he entered it.

"I do forgive you, Nick dear, as I hope to be forgiven by the Master for the wrongs I have done others - the wrong of accepting your life - in coldness," I answered, looking him steadily in the eye as I made my simple declaration of my new-found faith to him.

"You?" he faltered. "Do I behold you entered into the creed?"

"Listen to me, Nick, for the time is short," I said, as I held his hand close in mine. "We were blind - blind. When you and the children were in that death house I found that I must ask help. I cried out in my blindness and was answered, as Christ gave his promise that the eyes of those who ask should be opened. And you must ask so that you will have a vision to help - help you go to the blessed immortality that awaits you. Ask, Oh, Nick, ask with me. Please, Lord Jesus, help us!" And as I uttered my few faltering words of petition I fell on my knees beside the bed.

"It's too late now," he answered, but a helplessness came into his bitterness. "I've done all the damage I could and I'm not going to whimper. You'll help poor Martha?" he questioned softly, and I could have cried out in thankfulness for the ray of tenderness that came across his white face.

"God has given you time to right the worst wrong, Nick," I said, as a sudden thought came to me that gave to me a healing which I knew I must pour out upon his wounds. "Marry Martha and give the boy your name and your money to grow good and great with. Jacob is dead. They are alone in the world. Give them to me that way, Nick, give them to me to care for for you until we are all together where everything is made right."

For a long moment he lay perfectly still and looked into my eyes and I saw a wonder grow in his that spread all over his whole face.

"Some kind of a God must have created a woman like that in

Maria Thompson Daviess

you. Almost I believe. Call Goodloe quick, and your father."
And then he closed his eyes and I could see a deathly weakness
stealing over him. I called the nurse and sent her for father and
Gregory Goodloe, and to old Dabney who had come to wait
by the door I whispered to bring Martha and the boy and keep
them in the room beyond. Then I went back and knelt by the
pillow and took the hand which was beginning to grow cold in
mine.

"Could it be possible?" the white lips muttered.

"Say it, Nickols; say, 'Lord, help thou my unbelief,'" I begged
him.

"Amen," he whispered with a quick smile just as father and
Gregory Goodloe came into the room.

"Goodloe, what was the exact story about that skulker of a
thief on the cross?" Nickols asked with a sudden strength in his
voice as he opened his eyes and looked straight at the parson.

"'The thief said unto Jesus, "Lord, remember me when thou
comest into thy kingdom." And Jesus said unto him, "Verily I
say unto thee, to-day shalt thou be with me in Paradise,"' are
the exact words, Nickols," the parson answered him.

"Charlotte, ask the judge if he is willing that I should wipe the
slate clean as you propose in case there really is a door and an
old Peter to present a purified passport to," the dying man said
to me with a touch of his old whimsicality. "I give up, Greg;
the soul that Charlotte possesses can't be put out into
nothingness; and if she's got one I have too," he said, after a
moment's fight for breath. "Hurry, all of you, to get my
passport made out and bring the girl here to me. Quick, get
her. There is very little time."

"She's here, Nick," I answered, and after a few words to father
and the parson, to which they both gave assent, I called
Martha and the boy into the room.

Straight as a bird to its nest Martha flew to the bedside and the dying arms found strength to lift themselves and take her and the child into their embrace.

"Will you forgive me and let me make it as right with the world for you and him as I can, Martha?" he asked. "I love you, but I'd have drawn us all down into hell."

"Oh, no, no!" exclaimed Martha, looking up at me with positive fear of me and of father and of our world in her wild face.

"Yes, Martha," I said, as I knelt beside her and took the Stray in my arms, toward which he in his terror at the scene strained. "Father is a justice and he'll make the license over there in the desk right. You must, Martha, you must! It gives you and the boy to me to care for."

"Yes, Martha," echoed Nickols' voice, out of which the strength was quickly going. "Help me wipe off as much of the slate as you can," and the wandering hand suddenly encountered the boy's wee paddie resting on the edge of the bed and clasped it close.

And with the three of us crouched there beside him, father and Mr. Goodloe bound them legally and in the name of God, just as the last flicker of strength flared up in Nickols' body. Immediately I rose with the child in my arms and Martha took Nickols' head on her faithful breast while the life ebbed away.

"Amen, Charlotte, amen," were his last whispered words and I understood that he was ratifying again my prayer for light to lead the way of his faltering steps.

And then came a stillness in which we all stood with bowed heads while Martha sobbed.

The death of Nickols Morris Powers was an event of national interest and telegrams and letters and representatives of the press poured into Goodloets from all parts of the country. Mr. Jeffries and the Governor stayed with us until it was all over, and when Mr. Jeffries left he pressed into father's hand a large check of five figures.

"To help them build again, those who need it, in memory of him," he said.

The Governor and his staff spent time and effort in helping to reorganize Goodloets, but through it all it was the powerful Harpeth Jaguar on whom we all leaned. He came and went day and night, tireless, quiet, commanding, and with that great light shining from back of his eyes upon us all. And in his ministrations down in the Settlement he took Martha with him day after day. He forced her to use up all of the strength that she possessed each day so that she would drop with exhaustion at night. To me he left most of the comforting of Nell - and Harriet. Like all women of buoyant and shallow nature, Nell soon began to rebound from her tragedy and it was hard to keep Billy within decorous bounds in his comforting of her. It would have been impossible to have done it at all with the former Billy, but the quiet, steady light that shone in his honest eyes whenever he helped with Nell and the children spoke well for a reformed and perfectly satisfactory future for them all.

"Billy," I said to him one afternoon when he had taken all four of the kiddies out in his car to get wild grapes, when Harriet had counted on having wee Susan to herself for the afternoon, while Nell was interestedly busy over somber but much needed winter clothes for herself. "You have just got to make up your mind that Harriet is going to absolutely possess Sue for the future. I don't know about any legalities but I am going to see that Harriet gets Susan."

"What you say goes, Charlotte, as it always has," he answered me, with honest adoring in his young eyes that had lost their reckless hunger. "And if you aren't careful you'll lead us all into Kingdom Come in blind bridles. Be careful not to overfill Goodloe's fold. I don't want to crowd you. I'll take my turn when it comes." He was laughing as he spoke but there was a depth to the laughter that I understood.

"Thank you, Billy, for your consideration," I answered him, as I took small Sue's hand and turned in at the Sproul gate.

Harriet sat on the steps in the fading sunlight and the small music box flung herself into the outstretched arms with a force that was alarming. It was easy to see that Susan was most temperamental and would be a handful of anxieties in the years to come, anxieties that Harriet needed.

"Of course, she doesn't belong to me and I'm a fool," Harriet muttered as Susan darted away to see what treasure for her lurked in the pocket of Mrs. Sproul's beflowered silk skirt.

"I started plans to get her for you, just five minutes ago, dear," I said, as I sat down beside her. "I laid down the law to Billy on the subject."

"Charlotte," answered Harriet, as she looked with brooding into my eyes, "do you really believe that - that we will find them again and - and - *do* you really believe?" And the question was so hungry and haunted and so like what had driven me for years that my heart ached in my breast for her, but I knew that I could only stand fast and pray that she be comforted. I couldn't make her see.

"Yes, dear, I *know* - but I can't make you know. Just go on - on *hungering* like you are and you'll be fed," I answered.

"You've always understood, Charlotte, and if you say that the pain will some day be eased I'll - I'll believe it. Yes, I'll make a start by believing in you and there's no telling where it will land me."

The confidence with which she raised her comforted eyes to mine made a stab of pain hit me full in the breast. Words that

Gregory Goodloe had spoken to me out under the old graybeards were the weapon used. "With your hand in mine I can make this whole community see and know; separated from you -" In all humility I now understood what he meant.

And in all the weeks in which he and I had worked together Gregory Goodloe had given me not one single personal word or look. The priest had comforted and strengthened me but the man had forever shut me out of his heart. My suffering was intense, and yet, and yet I knew that in my heart there was strength to endure the want of him with all cheerfulness even to the end. At last I had found the key to my own hieroglyphics and I could be honest with myself. I knew that I loved Gregory Goodloe as it is seldom given to a woman to love a man, but I also knew that the awakening of spirit I had found was not in any way connected with my woman's love for him, but had come to me from the years of suffering I had had while I sought it. I refused to acknowledge that a sex spark had in any way set off the blaze; the fire had been laid in my soul and it would burn on without any of his tending. But even in that honest surety Nickols' mocking words "religion is suppressed sex" haunted me. I knew it could not be true, so I put it all out of my mind as I left Harriet and walked down the street towards the Poplars.

I was due in the library to help father in the packing of some of his papers, for I had insisted that he go on to Washington to fulfill his appointment. Martha and the boy would be with me and if he only left me Dabney I could be safe and busy for the winter. Strange to say, Mammy's disappointment at Dabney's loss of a sojourn in a strange clime was greater than his own.

"I don't believe in glorifying men by needing of them to any great measure," she declared. "With me in the house and the preacher across the fence it don't make no difference how good looking you are, Miss Charlotte, you won't be too much for our protection. Dabney can jest go on with the jedge."

"Of course, little miss, you don't need me, but I sorter got rheumatics in my homesick and I begged off from Mas' Nickols," Dabney replied with the wily soothing that had made his conjugal life both pleasant and possible.

I was thinking of the argument and smiled with tenderness as I saw the old grizzled white head bent over a hoe down in the dahlias, which he was bedding. The young man from White Plains had stayed to put the garden to bed as far as possible, and had left with perfect confidence in Dabney and the likely yellow boy he had found.

And now in late October the garden was in a conflagration of blossoming glory. The borders of the walks blazed with the red and blue and gold and purple of chrysanthemums and asters and zinnias and dahlias, while long tendrils of russet autumn vines trailed in and over and around the flowers and shrubs and hedges. The tang of ripening and falling seed was mixed in all the perfume, and gorgeous leaves were beginning to rustle on the green grass. It was Nickols' first harvest of beauty, and somehow I felt that there was no need to regret that his eyes were not mortally there to gather the fruits.

I went from the front porch up to my room to take off my hat and see if Martha had come from a day with Mother Spurlock down in the Settlement. I found instead of Martha or the boy or Mother Elsie, Jessie Litton seated at my desk and looking out the window across to Paradise Ridge.

"I came up to wait, Charlotte, because - because I'm in deep water and need a hand out. You have always helped and somehow I feel that you have so much more to give me now than you ever had. Clifton Gray told me last night that he loved me and is going to break his engagement with Letitia Cockrell. He had heard Letitia and Nell talk over Nell's mourning trousseau for the winter and he was disgusted - that, and - and I think it has been coming some time. He is with Mr. Goodloe a lot lately in getting things about the town started to going again and he is - is thinking. I don't know how to help him think; it's a thing I've never done. I am at sea myself but I know that he must not throw Letitia over. Will you talk to him?"

"I couldn't help him if - if Mr. Goodloe can't," I faltered, simply sick with distress.

"Cliff said not a week ago that your eyes made him feel like a light he saw ahead on a wooded island after he had drifted without a paddle two days in a canoe one time in Canada. You'll have to talk to him. Give him a little life kernel; I've only got shells for myself. I'm going down to Florida suddenly next week and when I come back I - I, well, I'll either go into the movies or study with Mother Spurlock to get a deaconess' cap." As she spoke I saw that the fight was on in Jessie's soul, and it would be to a finish.

"God bless and keep you, dear," I held her back long enough to say as she picked up her sweater and left me. Hampton Dibrell has been constantly with Bessie Thornton since Ted Montgomery's death, and I knew that Jessie's time of trial had come, for her love for him had grown through her denial because of the taint of her mad mother. And somehow I felt sure of the outcome, that she would find strength to let him go. I didn't know why I felt so sure; but I did, and I went down to the library with a great peace in my heart that I knew later would be in hers.

And I made my entry into father's den in the midst of a scene of great moment. I paused and listened with profound respect. Tradition was on trial and the result I felt would be momentous. Father sat in his huge chair before a small crackling fire in the wide chimney, and Martha's boy stood before him with a large, profusely illustrated volume of Hans Christian Andersen clasped passionately to his little breast. He had the floor.

"And Charlotte said they is no fairies anywhere and I say they is," he declaimed, while father listened attentively. Suddenly I saw what I had never seen before, that father's white hair rose in a crest on one side and descended in a cascade on the other at exactly the same angle as the black locks of the young arguer before him, and as they calmly regarded each other I thought I had never seen such a likeness in personality as well as form of feature. Love flooded all over me and I wanted to hug them both but was restrained to silence by the gravity of the situation.

"And why did you argue that there are fairies?" father interrogated calmly and judicially.

"Charlotte said they ain't here 'cause she and me had never saw one, and I said, 'How could a book and pictures be about nothing at all?' I showed her this book that Lady gaved me and she said, 'Maybe, but ask Minister.' I said, no, I'd ask you 'cause you are older and mighter saw one onct. Did you?"

"Well, sir, you argued from a positive, about ten pounds of positive, I should judge from the size of that volume, while Charlotte certainly argued from a negative viewpoint," said father, and his eyes twinkled as he gave me an almost imperceptible wink. By his answer he also avoided answering the question of faith put to him.

"Did you see one?" came back the question in a tone that demanded an answer.

"Here comes Minister now and you can ask him," father said in all cravenness as Mr. Goodloe came in the door behind me and came and stood at my side. He had a huge yellow plume of goldenrod which he handed me without looking at me directly. I buried my nose in its crispness and watched to see him meet the issue.

The boy put the question carefully just as he had put it to father, but there was a quaver in his voice as he ended with his plea.

"Is they no fairies, 'cause you can't see 'em?"

210   Maria Thompson Daviess

"Do you feel them in your heart?" was the counter question that came gravely from the lips of the Reverend Mr. Goodloe.

"Yes, here," answered the pleader as he laid his hand carefully on the pit of his stomach, which is nearer the seat of heartache than many a perturbed older person has come.

"Then for you there are fairies, right there in your heart, even if Charlotte has lost them out of hers," was the answer, with a theology that staggered me and set father smiling back into his youth.

"I'll go tell her and maybe give her some of mine," exclaimed the boy as he ran from the room.

CHAPTER XX

THE COVERT OF WINGS

"Oh, the faith of youth, the faith that reaches out to give itself," sighed father as he turned to his papers.

"Can faith give itself?" I asked, as I raised my eyes to the stars under dull gold through which Gregory Goodloe was pouring a great smile down into my depths.

"Sometimes - just sometimes I think that perhaps it can - it does," he answered me slowly and took my hands in his and held them with their palms together prayerwise, a thing he had done several times in the weeks past. Then he turned and walked over to father's desk and stood looking down at him.

"I want to dedicate the chapel on Sunday, Mr. Powers, as that is your last Sunday before you go to Washington," he said, and as he spoke he smiled first down into father's eyes raised to his and then into mine - impersonally. I couldn't trust myself to speak but turned and went up to my room to weep with a hurt that soon sent me to my knees, blind for the comfort that came - that I knew always would come now, no matter what the hurt.

"He knows it has come to me, and he's thankful - but he doesn't care," I sobbed and then laughed at my own contradictions.

Martha found me kneeling beside my window seat when she came in with Mother Spurlock and she shielded me until I could wipe away the tears and be as glad to see them both as I really was.

They were full of the plans for the dedication, which it gave me another stab to find they had been discussing with Mr. Goodloe for several days. In the hard weeks that had passed I had been their confidant, adviser and many times their helper in the reconstructing around the tragedies in the Settlement, but in this matter I had not been consulted. In fact, Mother Spurlock showed an embarrassed hesitation as she talked of it that still further hurt me and made me unenthusiastic and cold to their plans.

And why should I have been hurt that the surety in my heart had not declared itself to them without words? So wonderful did it seem to me that I thought it must be in my every word and deed and look and I was confounded that as yet I was considered to be an outsider and not entitled to plan for the ceremonial of the dedication of the material fold for the Reverend Mr. Goodloe's flock. And then suddenly my hurt was swept away by my sense of humor and I laughed to myself when I saw that to Mother Spurlock, who had hungered and thirsted for my conversion, I would have to prove it, tell it and repeat it.

"Instead of the festal ceremonies in the dedication Mr. Goodloe is going to have the simplest dedication ritual and then immediately hold the memorial services for our - our dead," said Mother Spurlock, as she took Martha's hand in hers and stroked it. "We want everybody to be there and I could use a few more of those trunks full of colored new clothes, Charlotte. The people down in the Settlement can use and wear after a dye pot when you can't, bless your sweet heart," and as she made her ruling request, which was still strong in death, she stroked the fold of dull black silk over my knee which was cut from the same material as the straight black widow's gown which Martha wore.

"Make Martha buy you some things for some of them," I said lightly and watched Martha as I spoke. She had never by word or deed showed that she felt anything but adoringly dependent on me and my bounty, and had put the check book I had given her from Mr. Cockrell away in my desk without looking at it. I could see that my words both hurt and shocked her.

"No, Oh, no," she faltered and turned away toward the window.

"But, Martha," I was beginning to say, when an interruption burst into the room. Young Charlotte stood before us and at her side the boy stood his ground with the huge book still in what must have been very tired arms. Their faces were belligerent and small James had upon his countenance the alarm he always shows during Charlotte's most serious and dangerous outbursts. Mikey was along, with his mischievous eyes dancing with delight at the fray.

"Auntie Charlotte, I think somebody ought to whip Stranger for saying that Minister said he had fairies in his stomach. It is a lie."

"I'll lick him fer you, Miss Charlotte," offered Mikey, with a pass at the boy that I knew was only an affectionate threat.

"I'll knock a stuffing out of you if you touch him," answered Charlotte, taking Mikey's offer with her usual literal directness. "When he's whipped, nobody but Auntie Charlotte can do it. Are you going to do it now, Auntie Charlotte? We don't want the devil to get him for badness." And as she spoke she took the boy's hand and held it tightly as if willing to defend him from the flesh, the devil and the world, only excepting myself.

"But he did say that I had them here when I put my hand on it, didn't he, Lady?" demanded the accused, with more courage than I would have felt at meeting the accusation for him. I simply couldn't face the explanation and I became craven.

Maria Thompson Daviess

"Mr. Goodloe is down in the library. Go ask him what he did say," I suggested hopefully.

"We looked everywhere for him and that is the place we skipped. I felt sure you wouldn't know anything at all about it, Auntie Charlotte, but Stranger said you know just as much as Minister, which is another thing I am going to ask him about. Come on, Stranger." And with her usual lightning rapidity, Charlotte began to marshal her forces out of the room.

"Please don't!" were the words I sent faltering after her determination to question Mr. Goodloe about his and my relative erudition, but I felt that they made no impression.

"Sonny thinks about you just as Charlotte does about Mr. Goodloe, and he'll say so to everybody," said Martha, with a sad smile after the door had closed with vigor enough to startle the household.

"He's a fine child," said Mother Spurlock, with a great tenderness in her smile at Martha. "Did you ask Mrs. Todd if that big hulk of a Jones boy could get into the coat that Dabney got me from the judge's closet?" she said, continuing the subject in hand, which lasted her for another hour. When she went she took Martha with her to carry half the bundles down to the Little House, the roof of which was the first thing to be patched in stricken Goodloets.

That night I felt the hands of the Stray on my face in the darkness and his soft cheek cuddle to mine.

"*You* say they *is* fairies, Lady," he coaxed.

"There are fairies and there always will be for you," I answered, as I drew him close and kissed the fragrant mouth so near mine. "Go back to mother now," I added, as I felt the sleepy huddle of his little shoulder against mine. He went and I promised myself that no matter how lonely I was to be I would always send him back to his mother and not ever forget that her claim was first. Tears were in my eyes as I turned my face into the pillow, but suddenly the refrain of the song I had once heard in the night, "Abide with me, fast falls the eventide," sung itself in my heart until I again fell to sleep.

The dedication day for Goodloe Chapel arrived upon Goodloets just one month from the day upon which the beast of storm had ravaged it, and as that fateful morning dawned with an extraordinary grandeur, so that Sunday in mid-October came up from behind Paradise Ridge with unusual beauty, only with the difference of calmness instead of splendor and peace instead of tumult. The sun was warm and benignant, with not a cloud in the deep blue sky to obscure its blessing. A gentle breeze blew in from the fields and meadows laden with rich harvest odors and every shrub and flower and vine which had been hiding back a few late buds let them burst forth in honor of the day, and in many instances they bloomed from a new growth thrown over the scars in the sides of the old town. In one short month most of the ruins had been reduced to orderly piles of material to be used in rebuilding, and a great many of the deepest gashes had been healed completely and covered with merciful vine and blossom. And it had also been like that with most of the scars in the lives of the bereaved; they ached, but they had been covered with a courage to go on building again until the new structure could be complete.

I think something of this feeling was in the minds of most of the people as they began to assemble around Goodloe Chapel long before the time for its opening. And as had happened once before, the procession from the Town met the procession from the Settlement, only this time they were not divided so completely from the right to the left. A tall mill woman, whose husband had gone down in the crash at the saddlery, came and took Nell's hand in hers and laid a strong arm around her shoulders, while Harriet went over and took from the arms of the young father the little motherless mite who had been res-cued from the pillow floating on the river. Billy shook hands with a young tanner in tight but wholly new clothes, to whom Luella May Spain introduced him as her imminent husband.

In times of stress women are apt to seize and cling to the arm of masculine protection, and Luella May had chosen to forget the fascination of Billy's hesitation and two-steps and secure for herself a life of thorough normality. She would probably never forget those dances with Billy, and they would lend a kind of reminiscent glow of pleasure over her boiling cabbage pots, but it would be no worse than that.

Mr. Todd was shaven and habitated in the neat black coat he had thrown off as he went at the ruin of the schoolhouse a month before, and with a tender smile on his lean old face he came over and stood beside Martha, as if to be watchful of her in the new order of her life.

And it was for quite a half hour that most of the inhabitants of Goodloets stood around in the yard of the chapel and waited for the formal opening of the doors. We all knew that the chapel would not hold the half of us, for the small Presbyterian congregation had been dismissed by Mr. Farraday to come over and join us in the dedication, and after a short service the boy Baptist divine had brought his flock to do honor to the opening of the new fold. In fact, by count almost every citizen in Goodloets stood before the chapel doors and waited for them to be thrown open. And in the crowd who waited there was this difference from the last time we had been together: All the children were with us and not separated from us by walls that crash. I think that the second meeting of Town and Settlement would have been impossible if each parent had not had the confidence inspired by the small hands in theirs.

And for still more minutes we were patient while the delicious autumn sun beamed upon us with Indian summer warmth and Old Harpeth looked down on us from out on Paradise Ridge with its crown wreathed with purple and gold and russet, all veiled in a tender haze.

Then as the old clock on the courthouse up on the square boomed the hour of eleven, Dabney with ceremony opened wide the tall doors and stepped back into the shadow, Jefferson bowing and smiling behind him. With one accord the people started toward the door, and then everybody again stood still and seemed to be waiting for something.

I knew for what they waited and I took Martha's hand in mine, with the boy's in hers on the other side, and slowly we walked through the path made for us between our friends and neighbors and in at the chapel door. As I passed Harriet I motioned to her and she put her arm around Nell and followed us, while Billy came behind them with father and the children. And behind them walked all of those who had been bereaved by the storm, and those who had been lamed and were suffering came with them.

My entry into the chapel had been accomplished and I felt like a storm-torn bird who finds its sanctuary among the green leaves of a great tree, while with Martha and the boy I went up to the very chancel rail itself.

Then I lifted my eyes and looked up into Gregory Goodloe's face, from which the white light of a great joy tinged with a great sorrow, looked down upon us. And as had been the case for all the long weeks stretched out behind me there was in his eyes no glance to me of a personal understanding; all the passion was that of a shepherd for his flock, and in its greatness I humbly acquiesced as I fell upon my knees in the front pew with Martha beside me, while he lifted his hands for the opening prayer of his service.

And in his short prayer he made the dedication of the pile of stone and mortar which had stood before the face of the wind as sturdily as old Harpeth itself. His words held the simplicity of those of a great poet and each was a separate jewel that could be imbedded in the hearts of his people to last for the span of their lives. He made a grateful acknowledgment of the safety of the chapel and of the spared lives of those before him, and in a few ringing sentences he prayed that we all be delivered from the blindness of the prosperity which was upon us when the disaster had made us halt in our rush and give

Maria Thompson Daviess

time for brother to face and call upon brother in affliction. So ringing and vivid was the self-accusation of heedlessness in the few sentences when he dealt with the condition of all of us when sorrow had come upon us, that we all held our breath with almost a groan of conviction, and his promise of our humbled and contrite hearts was ratified with a breath of relief.

Then we rose from our knees and sat once more facing him while he stood before us and began to read the memorial services for our dead. And through the whole beautiful ritual he led us to the very words of triumph:

"Then shall be brought to pass the saying that is written;
Death is swallowed up in victory. O death, where is thy sting?
O grave, where is thy victory?"

The warmth in his beautiful voice and the light upon his face poured over us all with a healing that we knew would endure.

After the dedication prayer and the memorial service the old Presbyterian minister, whom we had all known and loved since infancy, talked tenderly and with great sympathy to us for a few minutes and the stammering young Baptist divine gave us an insight into a heart of youthful devoutness.

And then came my hour.

"And now that we have given to the Lord formally this sanctuary we have builded for him, I want to open its spiritual doors to any of you who feel in your hearts the desire to unite with us in our worship of Him," were the words of invitation that I suddenly felt beat themselves, in the rich voice of the man in the pulpit, upon my heart. "I am going to baptize the children, but are there any of you of 'riper years' who desire to unite with us to 'constantly believe God's holy word, and obediently keep his commandments'?" And as he spoke he came down from the pulpit, stood at the chancel rail and stretched out his hands to all of us. Without a second's delay I rose and went and knelt before him and bowed my head in my hands. On my right knelt the young tanner and on my left I felt rather than saw Clifton Gray.

"The Ministration of Baptism to such as are of Riper Years" is long and full of holy austerity. Word for word, response for question, I followed the rich voice leading me, but not until it asked concerning our faith in the "life everlasting" did I raise my eyes to those glowing above me as I made answer:

"All this I steadfastly believe."

There was an instant's hush in the church as I made my response and in all humility I seemed to feel that it reverberated in some of the others' depths until it waked a faint echo. They had seen me face my humiliation and had watched how I took it and it had had its effect. It was as if I publicly led them to the well-spring of my courage and offered it to them. Luella May stole forward and crowded in between the young tanner and me, and I saw great tears steal out of father's closed eyes and roll down his cheeks, as he came and knelt just behind me, with two mill hands and several women.

And then, after our blessing, while we rose and stood on the right and the left of the chancel the parson asked that the children be brought forward for baptism.

Without waiting for anybody to come with her, Charlotte rose, took a hand of Sue on one side and one of Jimmy on the other, and came and stood looking up into the beloved Minister's eyes with such a vision in her young face that I caught my breath. Then Nell came and with her came Harriet with the Suckling asleep in her arms. The bereaved young father held his baby in his arms alone and Mrs. Burns went and stood beside him with Mikey and Maudie and the other five toddlers in front of her. Other children were brought forward by parents from the Town and the Settlement and were ranged to the right and to the left, but still I saw that Martha cowered in her pew holding the hand of the Stray in

Maria Thompson Daviess

hers as he knelt beside her. Then I knew what I must do and I went quietly and lifted her and led her to the chancel to a place just beside where Harriet stood with the Suckling in her arms. I held one of the Stray's little hands in mine, and young Charlotte dropped Jimmy's hand and reached out and took the other in hers. So we stood and waited while the beloved voice read through the beautiful ceremony with which children are taken into the arms of their faith before they are yet ready to understand what it is some day to mean to them.

"It is your duty to teach him ... to obediently keep God's holy will and commandments all of his life," were the closing words of the address with which the parson looked us full in the eye and laid the vow upon our souls. Then he reached out his hands, drew the Stray to him first, encircled him with his strong arm, laid his hands on the bowed black head, and looking me straight in the eye asked the question of his ritual:

"Name this child."

For an instant I glanced at Martha and then at father standing beside me, and as he nodded I slightly bent my head and into a deathly stillness all over the chapel I let the name fall clear and distinct:

"Nickols Morris Powers."

A beautiful ray of light flooded from one of the tall windows over both of us as he ratified the name with a few drops of water upon the boy's brow, and then turned to Harriet and repeated his question while he took the Suckling into his arms with the greatest tenderness. Then through the group he went, naming his lambs as he held them against his heart or within the circle of his strong arm. It was all so tender and so beautiful that every eye in the chapel was wet with tears and sobs echoed softly through his last prayer.

However, at one time in the ceremonial there was danger of a laugh from the aggregate, overwrought nerves when Charlotte promptly named herself without waiting for Nell's response which came late but in time to save embarrassment.

Then it was all over and the whole congregation trooped but into the sunshine. Father walked home with young Nickols on one side and Charlotte on the other, Martha carrying the Suckling and walking beside Harriet, who led Sue past the destruction of her white dress which every mud puddle threatened. Cliff Gray came with me slowly up the street after all the others had gone ahead and most of them had turned into the gates of their respective homes.

"Is everything all right now, Cliff?" I questioned him, as we walked slowly under the old elms of our ancestors' planting. "It is all right now?" I asked again, while Cliff looked off into the distance.

"I have faith that I can make it that way now, Charlotte dear," he answered, as I paused to turn in at my gate. We clasped hands for a second and then he went on down the street toward the Cockrell gate; and Letitia's material point of view on existence I knew would have a fair chance at his hands.

I felt that I had never loved my friends as I did that wonderful Sunday, and I hoped it would not bore them if I at times let some of it overflow into their well ordered lives.

The rest of that long, hazy, dreamy, wonder day, in the morning of which our hearts had been poured so full, we all of us spent with father, as he was to leave us the next morning. Against the remonstrance of his maternal parent, the worthless Jefferson had been chosen to go along in the place of his father Dabney. The young negro's brisk packings filled the house with a joy note that was delightful and Mammy admonished him on subjects moral every time he came near the kitchen.

Late in the afternoon I left father down in the garden with young Nickols, to whom he was confiding the care of some very choice hollyhock seeds that would need gathering in the next few weeks.

"Your father got them from England," the judge said gravely, as he showed the small paddies how to roll out the thin seed without crushing them.

"Have I got any father but the Lady?" asked the youngster with all seriousness, as he beamed up in my direction. Suddenly Martha turned and went indoors and up to her room. I followed her and sat down beside the bed on which she had flung herself.

"You'll have to make him understand it all; I can't," she said, after I had tenderly hushed her weeping. "I give him to you. I - I won't be with him long." As she spoke I noticed how the light shone through her pale fingers as she held them up to clasp mine.

"We'll go away to Florida for a rest, Martha," I said, with the reassurance I found I had constantly to use to her. There was a great and beautiful tenderness in the soul of Martha, but she was completely lacking in any of the worldly initiative that makes lives move on. She seemed to be standing still.

"Yes, I'll go away," she answered softly, as she unclasped her hand from mine, nestled her face in the pillow and shut her eyes.

I left her to sleep and a year from that hour I knew that I had not understood the measure of her exhaustion. She faded like a flower and drifted on into eternity like a gossamer thread in the breeze.

And it was with some of the depression that a kind of maternal brooding over her gave me that I went out into the garden that night after all the rest had gone to bed. A pale silver moon-crescent poised on the brow of Old Harpeth and a tingling little breeze was coming down from the north as if sent as a warning of the winter soon to be upon us. I went down to the old graybeard poplars and their leaves seemed to hiss together in the moonlight instead of rustling softly as they had been all summer. A great many of them were drifted in dry waves on the grass and their gold was turned to silver in the moonlight. Many of the tall shrubs were naked ghosts of their former selves and gnashed their bones drearily. I leaned against the tallest old poplar and looked out across the valley with a kind of stillness in my heart that seemed to be listening and then listening.

"Oh, I'm thankful, thankful that strength has been given me to endure it all - life," I said to myself, almost under my breath. "And no matter what comes I can never lose it. I can go out into life now alone and - unafraid."

"'And whither thou goest I too will go, and thy -'" came the Gregorian chant from close beside me, and I turned to find the Harpeth Jaguar stalking me in the night.

Then for a long time we stood and looked at each other, he tearing away the veil from his man's heart and I laying aside that in my woman's breast.

"Oh, I've needed you so," I finally said, with a catch in my breath as I put my hands in his which he put palm to palm, then raised to his lips.

"You were in God's hands and I had to wait His time," he answered me. "And I would have waited until the stars burn dim. As near as loss came I never doubted. I had asked Him for you."

"I didn't know I was going to join your church this morning," I faltered. "I never intended to join your church. I was going to be either a Baptist or a Presbyterian. I was afraid to mix - my faith with - with you."

"Hasn't it been tried sufficiently to stand any test? I think so. Ah, dear, come to me - it's been long for me, too." His arms entreated me, but I held myself away with my praying hands pressed to his breast.

"Are you sure that I'm not mixing you and - your faith?" I asked, looking him honestly in the face and giving voice to the thought that Nickols had put into my mind and which had tortured me all the weary months past.

"Did any thought of me make you bring Martha Ensley to Nickols' death bed and take into your heart and home what the world calls dishonor?"

"No," I answered with honesty to myself.

"Have you once since you knew - *knew* - felt that you must turn to me for comfort and help in one of your dire hours?"

"Not once," I answered again with honesty.

"Have you not learned to turn to Him?"

"I have!" I answered.

"That's God's love. Then you can give me the love that belongs to me in your heart's kingdom, can't you?"

"I'm afraid - I'm going to love you too much - I feel it coming. What'll you do with it? Stop me!" I said with both a sob and a laugh, as I began to let myself be drawn into the strong, hungry arms.

"You great, big, splendid woman of God! You've got love enough in you to feed a multitude and you'll do it. Give me a part of my share now. It's mine. God sent you to me; I'm going to take you."

And he did. His lips pressed mine until I gave back a betrothal kiss that was as complete as a great red flower. His arms held me so that they were a circle of pain, but all the while I kept my hands prayerwise between the clamor of our breasts.

"Say it - 'the covert of thy wings' - all that David said," I whispered.

And he answered:

"'I will abide in thy tabernacle forever: I will trust in the covert of thy wings.'"

Choose from Thousands of 1stWorldLibrary Classics By

A. M. Barnard	C. M. Ingleby	Elizabeth Gaskell
Ada Leverson	Carolyn Wells	Elizabeth McCracken
Adolphus William Ward	Catherine Parr Traill	Elizabeth Von Arnim
Aesop	Charles A. Eastman	Ellem Key
Agatha Christie	Charles Amory Beach	Emerson Hough
Alexander Aaronsohn	Charles Dickens	Emilie F. Carlen
Alexander Kielland	Charles Dudley Warner	Emily Dickinson
Alexandre Dumas	Charles Farrar Browne	Enid Bagnold
Alfred Gatty	Charles Ives	Enilor Macartney Lane
Alfred Ollivant	Charles Kingsley	Erasmus W. Jones
Alice Duer Miller	Charles Klein	Ernie Howard Pie
Alice Turner Curtis	Charles Hanson Towne	Ethel May Dell
Alice Dunbar	Charles Lathrop Pack	Ethel Turner
Allen Chapman	Charles Romyn Dake	Ethel Watts Mumford
Ambrose Bierce	Charles Whibley	Eugenie Foa
Amelia E. Barr	Charles Willing Beale	Eugene Wood
Amory H. Bradford	Charlotte M. Braeme	Eustace Hale Ball
Andrew Lang	Charlotte M. Yonge	Evelyn Everett-green
Andrew McFarland Davis	Charlotte Perkins Stetson	Everard Cotes
Andy Adams	Clair W. Hayes	F. H. Cheley
Anna Alice Chapin	Clarence Day Jr.	F. J. Cross
Anna Sewell	Clarence E. Mulford	F. Marion Crawford
Annie Besant	Clemence Housman	Federick Austin Ogg
Annie Hamilton Donnell	Confucius	Ferdinand Ossendowski
Annie Payson Call	Coningsby Dawson	Francis Bacon
Annie Roe Carr	Cornelis DeWitt Wilcox	Francis Darwin
Annonaymous	Cyril Burleigh	Frances Hodgson Burnett
Anton Chekhov	D. H. Lawrence	Frances Parkinson Keyes
Arnold Bennett	Daniel Defoe	Frank Gee Patchin
Arthur Conan Doyle	David Garnett	Frank Harris
Arthur M. Winfield	Dinah Craik	Frank Jewett Mather
Arthur Ransome	Don Carlos Janes	Frank L. Packard
Arthur Schnitzler	Donald Keyhoe	Frank V. Webster
Atticus	Dorothy Kilner	Frederic Stewart Isham
B.H. Baden-Powell	Dougan Clark	Frederick Trevor Hill
B. M. Bower	Douglas Fairbanks	Frederick Winslow Taylor
B. C. Chatterjee	E. Nesbit	Friedrich Kerst
Baroness Emmuska Orczy	E.P.Roe	Friedrich Nietzsche
Baroness Orczy	E. Phillips Oppenheim	Fyodor Dostoyevsky
Basil King	Earl Barnes	G.A. Henty
Bayard Taylor	Edgar Rice Burroughs	G.K. Chesterton
Ben Macomber	Edith Van Dyne	Gabrielle E. Jackson
Bertha Muzzy Bower	Edith Wharton	Garrett P. Serviss
Bjornstjerne Bjornson	Edward Everett Hale	Gaston Leroux
Booth Tarkington	Edward J. O'Biren	George A. Warren
Boyd Cable	Edward S. Ellis	George Ade
Bram Stoker	Edwin L. Arnold	Geroge Bernard Shaw
C. Collodi	Eleanor Atkins	George Durston
C. E. Orr	Eliot Gregory	George Ebers

George Eliot
George Gissing
George MacDonald
George Meredith
George Orwell
George Sylvester Viereck
George Tucker
George W. Cable
George Wharton James
Gertrude Atherton
Gordon Casserly
Grace E. King
Grace Gallatin
Grace Greenwood
Grant Allen
Guillermo A. Sherwell
Gulielma Zollinger
Gustav Flaubert
H. A. Cody
H. B. Irving
H.C. Bailey
H. G. Wells
H. H. Munro
H. Irving Hancock
H. Rider Haggard
H. W. C. Davis
Haldeman Julius
Hall Caine
Hamilton Wright Mabie
Hans Christian Andersen
Harold Avery
Harold McGrath
Harriet Beecher Stowe
Harry Castlemon
Harry Coghill
Harry Houidini
Hayden Carruth
Helent Hunt Jackson
Helen Nicolay
Hendrik Conscience
Hendy David Thoreau
Henri Barbusse
Henrik Ibsen
Henry Adams
Henry Ford
Henry Frost
Henry James
Henry Jones Ford
Henry Seton Merriman
Henry W Longfellow
Herbert A. Giles

Herbert Carter
Herbert N. Casson
Herman Hesse
Hildegard G. Frey
Homer
Honore De Balzac
Horace B. Day
Horace Walpole
Horatio Alger Jr.
Howard Pyle
Howard R. Garis
Hugh Lofting
Hugh Walpole
Humphry Ward
Ian Maclaren
Inez Haynes Gillmore
Irving Bacheller
Isabel Hornibrook
Israel Abrahams
Ivan Turgenev
J.G.Austin
J. Henri Fabre
J. M. Barrie
J. Macdonald Oxley
J. S. Fletcher
J. S. Knowles
J. Storer Clouston
Jack London
Jacob Abbott
James Allen
James Andrews
James Baldwin
James Branch Cabell
James DeMille
James Joyce
James Lane Allen
James Lane Allen
James Oliver Curwood
James Oppenheim
James Otis
James R. Driscoll
Jane Austen
Jane L. Stewart
Janet Aldridge
Jens Peter Jacobsen
Jerome K. Jerome
John Burroughs
John Cournos
John F. Kennedy
John Gay
John Glasworthy

John Habberton
John Joy Bell
John Kendrick Bangs
John Milton
John Philip Sousa
Jonas Lauritz Idemil Lie
Jonathan Swift
Joseph A. Altsheler
Joseph Carey
Joseph Conrad
Joseph E. Badger Jr
Joseph Hergesheimer
Joseph Jacobs
Jules Vernes
Julian Hawthrone
Julie A Lippmann
Justin Huntly McCarthy
Kakuzo Okakura
Kenneth Grahame
Kenneth McGaffey
Kate Langley Bosher
Kate Langley Bosher
Katherine Cecil Thurston
Katherine Stokes
L. A. Abbot
L. T. Meade
L. Frank Baum
Latta Griswold
Laura Dent Crane
Laura Lee Hope
Laurence Housman
Lawrence Beasley
Leo Tolstoy
Leonid Andreyev
Lewis Carroll
Lewis Sperry Chafer
Lilian Bell
Lloyd Osbourne
Louis Hughes
Louis Tracy
Louisa May Alcott
Lucy Fitch Perkins
Lucy Maud Montgomery
Luther Benson
Lydia Miller Middleton
Lyndon Orr
M. Corvus
M. H. Adams
Margaret E. Sangster
Margret Howth
Margaret Vandercook

Margret Penrose
Maria Edgeworth
Maria Thompson Daviess
Mariano Azuela
Marion Polk Angellotti
Mark Overton
Mark Twain
Mary Austin
Mary Catherine Crowley
Mary Cole
Mary Hastings Bradley
Mary Roberts Rinehart
Mary Rowlandson
M. Wollstonecraft Shelley
Maud Lindsay
Max Beerbohm
Myra Kelly
Nathaniel Hawthrone
Nicolo Machiavelli
O. F. Walton
Oscar Wilde
Owen Johnson
P.G. Wodehouse
Paul and Mabel Thorne
Paul G. Tomlinson
Paul Severing
Percy Brebner
Peter B. Kyne
Plato
R. Derby Holmes
R. L. Stevenson
R. S. Ball
Rabindranath Tagore
Rahul Alvares
Ralph Bonehill
Ralph Henry Barbour
Ralph Victor
Ralph Waldo Emmerson
Rene Descartes
Rex Beach

Rex E. Beach
Richard Harding Davis
Richard Jefferies
Richard Le Gallienne
Robert Barr
Robert Frost
Robert Gordon Anderson
Robert L. Drake
Robert Lansing
Robert Lynd
Robert Michael Ballantyne
Robert W. Chambers
Rosa Nouchette Carey
Rudyard Kipling
Samuel B. Allison
Samuel Hopkins Adams
Sarah Bernhardt
Sarah C. Hallowell
Selma Lagerlof
Sherwood Anderson
Sigmund Freud
Standish O'Grady
Stanley Weyman
Stella Benson
Stella M. Francis
Stephen Crane
Stewart Edward White
Stijn Streuvels
Swami Abhedananda
Swami Parmananda
T. S. Ackland
T. S. Arthur
The Princess Der Ling
Thomas A. Janvier
Thomas A Kempis
Thomas Anderton
Thomas Bailey Aldrich
Thomas Bulfinch
Thomas De Quincey
Thomas Dixon

Thomas H. Huxley
Thomas Hardy
Thomas More
Thornton W. Burgess
U. S. Grant
Valentine Williams
Various Authors
Vaughan Kester
Victor Appleton
Victoria Cross
Virginia Woolf
Wadsworth Camp
Walter Camp
Walter Scott
Washington Irving
Wilbur Lawton
Wilkie Collins
Willa Cather
Willard F. Baker
William Dean Howells
William le Queux
W. Makepeace Thackeray
William W. Walter
William Shakespeare
Winston Churchill
Yei Theodora Ozaki
Yogi Ramacharaka
Young E. Allison
Zane Grey

www.ingramcontent.com/pod-product-compliance
Lightning Source LLC
Chambersburg PA
CBHW020500100426
42813CB00030B/3062/J